SERIAL INNOVATORS

SERIAL INNOVATORS

*How Individuals Create and
Deliver Breakthrough Innovations
in Mature Firms*

Abbie Griffin,
Raymond L. Price,
and Bruce A. Vojak

STANFORD BUSINESS BOOKS
An Imprint of Stanford University Press
Stanford, California

Stanford University Press
Stanford, California

Special discounts for bulk quantities of Stanford Business Books
are available to corporations, professional associations, and other
organizations. For details and discount information, contact the special
sales department of Stanford University Press.
Tel: (650) 736-1782, Fax: (650) 736-1784

Printed in the United States of America on acid-free, archival-quality paper

Library of Congress Cataloging-in-Publication Data

Griffin, Abbie, author.
    Serial innovators : how individuals create and deliver breakthrough
innovations in mature firms / Abbie Griffin, Raymond L. Price, and Bruce
A. Vojak.
        pages cm
    Includes bibliographical references and index.
    ISBN 978-0-8047-7597-7 (cloth : alk. paper)
    1. Technological innovations—Management.   2. New products.
I. Price, Raymond L. (Raymond Lewis), author.   II. Vojak, Bruce A.,
author.   III. Title.
HD45.G69 2012
658.4'063—dc23
                                                            2011040724

Typeset by Newgen in 10/15 Sabon

We jointly dedicate this book to all the individuals and firms striving to make the world a better place through developing new technologies and products that provide improved solutions to problems that we have.

To John Horne, former CEO of Navistar International Truck and Engine, for starting me down this research path, my terrific son, Griffin Spotz, and my wonderful husband, Ken. —Abbie

To my wife, Stephanie, whose support and encouragement have made my contributions possible, and to my children and grandchildren, who provide great joy in my life. —Ray

To my wife and son, Deb and Andrew, with whom I continue to work out the reality that we love because He first loved us. S.D.G. —Bruce

CONTENTS

Preface and Acknowledgments   ix

Introduction: Serial Innovators and Why They Matter   1

1   Breakthrough Innovation in Mature Firms   14

2   The Processes by Which Serial Innovators Innovate   36

3   Customer Engagement for Breakthrough Innovation   70

4   Navigating the Politics of Breakthrough Innovation   89

5   Characteristics of Serial Innovators   112

6   Identifying and Developing Serial Innovators   135

7   Managing Serial Innovators for Impact   152

8   Love Letters to Our Customers: Serial Innovators, Aspiring Serial Innovators, and All Those with and for Whom They Work   183

Appendix: Interview Suggestions for Identifying Potential Serial Innovators   203

References   209

Index   213

PREFACE AND ACKNOWLEDGMENTS

This book is based on several years of academic research on Serial Innovators conducted by the coauthors and a number of graduate students. In conducting the research, we interviewed over fifty Serial Innovators and a larger number of their coworkers, managers, and human resource managers. These Innovators are some of the best product development people in the world. They graciously shared with us how they think, how they work, and how they create breakthrough new products. The interviews and other empirical studies helped us understand who these Serial Innovators are as people, how they innovate, what motivates them, and how best to manage them. If organizations are going to develop the breakthrough innovations that enable organic growth, they need to have these types of people and the structured space they need to perform their work. Serial Innovators' practices have significant implications for organization structure, investment, and management. If firms want to create breakthrough products in the future, these people provide the best models we have to understand what is required. The purpose of this book is to help people and corporations better understand, emulate, enable, support, and manage these unique and important individuals, who have the potential to create new breakthrough products that result in large revenue and profit streams, primarily for large, mature firms.

Several different types of people residing in large firms will benefit from reading this book:

PEOPLE WHO ALREADY ARE SERIAL INNOVATORS

- This book will help clarify to you what you do, how you do it, and why it is important to keep doing it.
- Our research may provide insight into how you can innovate even more effectively.
- Parts of this book may help you help others around you understand how you innovate and validate to them why you work and innovate the way you do, providing them insight into how to better collaborate with you or to manage you more effectively.

POTENTIAL FUTURE SERIAL INNOVATORS

- Our research will show you what additional knowledge and skill sets you may need to build to maximize your ability to successfully innovate in existing corporations.
- This book will help you inform your manager(s) on how to more effectively develop your capabilities.

COLLEAGUES OF SERIAL INNOVATORS— INVENTORS, CHAMPIONS, AND IMPLEMENTERS

- This book will help clarify the various roles that are important for developing new products.
- Our research will help you understand the importance of your work with and support of Serial Innovators.

TECHNOLOGY STUDENTS FOCUSED ON INNOVATION

- This book may help you determine what roles in creating new products that your intrinsic personality and perspectives are best suited for.
- Our research outlines the skills and capabilities that can be developed in order for you to have a productive career.

MANAGERS OF SERIAL INNOVATORS AND POTENTIAL SERIAL INNOVATORS

- Our research will help you identify potential future Innovators and provide you with the knowledge you need to nurture their potential.
- This book will help you lead these rare, but impactful, individuals more effectively.
- Our research will help you validate Serial Innovators' methods and potential impact to your senior management.

HUMAN RESOURCE MANAGERS

- This book will demonstrate to you how crucial Serial Innovators are for the success of your organization.
- This research will help you create organizations in which Serial Innovators can be accepted and will thrive.

TECHNICAL EXECUTIVES (CTOS) AND BUSINESS EXECUTIVES (CEOS, COOS, AND PRESIDENTS)

- This book will show you how Serial Innovators can be used as a mechanism in addition to technology push and marketing pull efforts to help your firm create successful breakthrough products that produce significant new revenue and profit.
- This research will help you structure your organization to more effectively support Serial Innovators' resource and management needs.

We thank each of the people who took time out of their busy schedules to talk with us and share their insights, knowledge, and feelings on these topics. We are indebted to each of you and hope that you are innovating away in a supportive and energizing environment. We wrote this book in the hope that it would help others achieve the kinds of new product accomplishments that you have, but perhaps with fewer organizational difficulties than those that some of you have encountered.

We also are indebted to our research assistants who worked in various aspects of the project over the years:

- Matthew Maloney, MS, General Engineering, 2003

- John Hebda, MS, Systems and Entrepreneurial Engineering, 2004

- Konstantin Perlov, MS, General Engineering, 2004

- Edward Sim, MS, Electrical Engineering, 2005

- Nathan Hoffman, MS, Systems and Entrepreneurial Engineering, 2007

- Matthew Marvel, PhD, Human Resources Education, 2007

- Allen Barton, MS, Systems and Entrepreneurial Engineering, 2009

- Holli Burgon, PhD, Education Psychology, 2009

We also would like to acknowledge the following organizations for their financial support of this research:

- Institute for the Study of Business Markets: http://isbm.smeal.psu.edu

- Marketing Science Institute: http://www.msi.org

- University of Illinois at Urbana-Champaign Campus Research Board: http://crb.research.illinois.edu/

Abbie Griffin, Salt Lake City, UT
Raymond L. Price, Champaign, IL
Bruce A. Vojak, Urbana, IL
November 2011

SERIAL INNOVATORS

INTRODUCTION
Serial Innovators and Why They Matter

Carol Bernick is a Serial Innovator.* As a marketing executive at the Alberto Culver Company in the 1980s, she invented first Mrs. Dash® Original Blend salt-free seasoning and then Molly McButter® fat-free butter flavoring. Mrs. Dash is now the most popular salt-free blend in the seasoning category, and the product line has been expanded to include a number of other salt-free seasonings, as well as salt-free marinades. These product lines constitute a significant portion of Alberto Culver's 2008 $84 million nonbeauty revenue stream.

Chuck House also is a Serial Innovator. While at Hewlett-Packard (HP), he invented a number of new products. Most noteworthy among them is the logic analyzer, which records bus communications between two semiconductor chips. Before logic analyzers, engineers used oscilloscopes to help them understand how the circuits they designed were functioning—one signal at a time, a tedious process. Because logic analyzers record many signals simultaneously, these devices drastically improved an engineer's ability to understand circuit operations, speeding the electronic development for myriad new products. In 2002, *Electronic Design Magazine* recognized the logic analyzer as one of the fifty most important

---

* Throughout this book, "Serial Innovators" is capitalized to emphasize the special role these individuals play in innovation.

electronic innovations ever developed. Since its invention, this product line has earned HP and Agilent hundreds of millions of dollars.

Serial Innovators are individuals who have conceived ideas that solve important problems for people and organizations, have developed those ideas into breakthrough new products and services, inventing new technologies to do so as needed, and then have guided those products and services through the corporation's commercialization process and into the market. Serial Innovators are important to corporations because, like Carol Bernick and Chuck House, they can develop products that generate millions of dollars of revenue. In doing so, Serial Innovators impact millions of lives every day, from the workers employed to make these breakthrough products to the customers who benefit from them. Frequently, Serial Innovators' products change the lives of millions of people for the better.

Serial Innovators in the "creative arts"—of which Paul McCartney is a great example—most frequently innovate independently or with a friend or two, without worrying about whether others in a corporation or firm will allow their ideas to come to fruition. Some Serial Innovators, like Steve Jobs, reside at the top of corporations and can dictate what product ideas the firm will pursue. Other Serial Innovators innovate in the context of entrepreneurial start-ups, like Martin Eberhard, who founded NuvoMedia to develop the Rocket eBook® and Tesla Motors to develop the Tesla Roadster® electric sports car. As founders of start-ups, these Serial Innovators also have significant authority in dictating the innovative path followed.

This book, however, is about Serial Innovators like Carol Bernick and Chuck House,* who reside in the middle levels of large, mature firms, successfully creating breakthrough innovations in spite of organizational systems that seem more likely to stymie breakthrough innovation than support it. These Serial Innovators cannot dictate what products the organization will develop. Instead, they have to use their interpersonal, organizational, and political skills—in addition to their business and technical skills—to bring their innovative visions to commercial fruition.

---

* Charles H. House has written an interesting book, *Permission Denied: Odyssey of an Intrapreneur from "The Medal of Defiance" to the Corporate Boardroom*, working copy June 2011.

Serial Innovators work differently from the typical development employee. Thus, they need to be managed differently. Although these employees can bring in huge revenue streams, their unconventional innovation processes and the way in which they navigate the politics of project acceptance are so different from the firm's formalized processes, they inherently cause problems for the organization. Consider the following Serial Innovator story.

TOM OSBORN: THE BILLION-DOLLAR PRODUCT THAT NEARLY WASN'T

Tom Osborn is a Serial Innovator at Procter & Gamble (P&G). In the early 1980s, he invented the technology behind the Always® Ultra feminine hygiene pad, one of P&G's billion-dollar (annual revenue) brands. But Tom's innovation nearly got him fired.

After earning a PhD in chemistry, Tom completed a postdoctoral fellowship in which he helped develop technology to measure cosmic ray–induced reactions on the moon—a safety aspect of the Apollo 17 lunar mission. Upon joining P&G, Tom worked in basic research, where he developed radiotracer and nuclear analytical methodologies, most of which also supported safety programs.

After four and a half years in basic research, Tom moved to a research and development (R&D) position in the business side of P&G, in the analytical section of the paper category. Historically, the company looked at paper process improvements in terms of the mechanical structures of papermaking, but Tom was inclined to consider chemical techniques instead. This unique perspective yielded some of his first patents.

Later in his career, when offered a position in P&G's feminine care category, also part of the paper group, Tom made the move. At the time Tom joined feminine care, the group was reorganizing. P&G believed that feminine hygiene offered great opportunities and wanted to enter the market rapidly with a new sanitary pad. The product was in the final stages of development. It featured a new, proprietary technology that had performed very well in its early consumer testing; everyone was excited about the launch.

But an issue with the adhesives that bonded the top sheet to the pad's absorbing core threatened the timeline. Tom quickly defined the problem and laid out a simple solution; development continued on track. The next step was a limited manufacturing run—just enough product to stage a test market in several cities. Tom was then asked to resolve another typical manufacturing issue. Again, he helped keep the pad moving toward launch.

When he was in basic research, Tom was free to approach problems from a holistic perspective; he was now being asked to work in a more directed way. As part of a business unit working on a new launch initiative, he was expected to solve specific technology issues. But the idea of looking at things from a narrower, technology-specific perspective ran counter to his orientation as a scientist. It was impossible for him to turn his curiosity off. Intuitively, he began to think of feminine pads within the wider context of menstruation—the process itself and the way it impacted women's lives.

He soon realized that the current pad reflected an engineering-based approach to solving women's problems associated with menstruation. The technical group had "made a device to catch fluid" without considering the properties of the fluid or the way the pad interacted with the body. Despite the fact that early consumer testing showed that the proprietary technology worked—the pad offered noticeable dryness as compared to competitive products—it did not perform well in other aspects, including comfort. The more time he spent on the initiative, the more Tom was convinced that "there was no substantial biological and physical science" behind the new pad.

Tom believed that P&G could develop a superior performing pad that was also comfortable, and that such a pad would make a significant difference in consumers' lives. Tom explains: "One of my primary goals in life was to be the most popular guy in the world with women. [*laughs*] But seriously, I really wanted to improve the quality of women's lives."

Tom's supervisor gave him the go-ahead to conduct the basic research needed to create a fundamental understanding of pad performance and to translate that understanding into a prototype product.

Tom's methods were a radical shift from the ways the product development group had approached research in the past. The fluid the team had been using to test prototypes bore little similarity to menstrual blood. Tom changed the testing and testing protocols to a blood-based substance, and that was just the beginning. He also analyzed wear and flow patterns on thousands of used pads, personally examining hundreds of pads himself. And he realized that, because the FDA classified pads as medical devices, many of the clinical methodologies used in medical device development could be applied to pad research. By building relationships with physicians and staff at a nearby medical school, he was able to investigate the physical and psychological aspects of menstruation, and to develop methodologies to learn how pads interact with and move on a woman's panty as she moves. The more he learned, the more he doubted the veracity of the prevailing model.

Tom knew that most of his product development colleagues came to feminine care from P&G's diaper category. He understood why their mental model of menstruation was, unconsciously, an extrapolation of learning based on diapers. He also understood why they thought of the pad as something that needed to capture and contain a thin, free-flowing stream of fluid. Tom's research showed that menstrual fluid was, in reality, a viscous fluid that was thicker than urine, and that it left the body slowly, through a combination of small drops and intermittent surges. He began to formulate a model built around a series of thicker drops being pulled from the body by gravity, drops that needed to be *pulled into* an interior absorptive pad core.

Through his research Tom became convinced that, in women's minds, product performance was about more than just leakage protection, which could be achieved simply by making the product bigger. Indeed, the approximate menstrual pad size at that time was one-inch thick by two-and-a-half-inches wide by six- to eight-inches long. Tom's extensive direct-user research indicated that women also wanted comfort, and that pads of the day were anything but comfortable. Women often described the experience as "wearing a brick."

Tom's medical school investigations showed that pad comfort included two aspects: thinness and flexibility. Even if P&G had been focused on comfort, it would have been difficult to achieve using the current technology platform, in which comfort improvements came at the expense of protection. The first Always product was now on the market and, although superior to competitive products, was designed strictly for leakage protection. It was not comfortable. Tom now was certain that the design basis was fundamentally flawed.

He also was convinced that he could invent a pad that would help women get through their monthly periods with increased confidence and ease. Using his new mental model, he began to visualize this pad, not as an absorbent brick, but as a replaceable panty crotch—a smaller, softer, thinner, and more flexible panty "liner." The pad Tom imagined would behave as a garment.

His timing could not have been worse. Although his supervisor had approved Tom's basic research, he hardly expected Tom would challenge the whole basis of the recently launched product and the entire follow-on upgrade program. Given the recently launched pad's competitively superior proprietary technology, everyone was committed to making it a success. Tom's holistic, radically different model also threatened a number of key managers at a deeper level. All had invested significant time and resources—not to mention their reputations—into the old model. Tom's push back was not well received.

Tom's manager ordered him to stop work on his model and to focus on delivering the current initiative. When Tom kept talking about his new comfort-based model and started developing prototypes, his manager began to view him as disruptive to the organization and started the termination process. His manager also eliminated Tom's technical support and other resources, leaving him only an office and a phone.

As long as he was going to be fired, Tom decided to keep working on the product he knew in his heart would transform the quality of life for many women. He found a discarded computer and got to work. Through his network of technical colleagues, Tom knew that the diaper organization was experimenting with superabsorbent materials, which would deliver high absorbency with far less bulk. After locating the new, thinner, absorbent material, he quickly realized that he had to create a laminated product. His pad needed a soft cover to allow the fluid to spread through the tissue layers, a superabsorbent core, and a thin, flexible bottom plastic sheet to prevent fluid from moving out of the pad and onto clothing.

Since the diaper organization could not supply a laminate structure that met his specifications, Tom worked with an external supplier to obtain a suitable laminate. Then he befriended a contract worker in the development organization who could hand-make pad prototypes. He asked female family and friends to test them. According to Tom, he was able to "bootleg" the prototype development because P&G's accounting systems in the early 1980s were not as "tight" as today. He believes it would be unlikely that anyone could pursue a similar path now. Importantly, Tom did not compromise on safety. He leveraged relationships with old friends in the safety organization to conduct proper evaluations and to provide clearance for testing.

The anecdotal data were encouraging: women loved the pads. But Tom knew he couldn't approach other managers without a statistical panel test. Because a large-scale panel test would require hundreds of pads, Tom and his contractor friend handmade an interim amount (the amount needed for a small-scale panel test) on bootleg.

Around this time, Tom fortuitously found himself under the supervision of a new manager. She was a scientist by training, so Tom hoped she might be open to alternative models. She was, and signed off on a formal test request. The results were stunning. Approximately 80% of the participants preferred Tom's thin, body-conforming pad to the current P&G product. It was a hands-down winner.

Still, the support of Tom's immediate manager was not enough. In the time since Tom had begun work on his alternate model, the feminine care business had realized great success with the initial pad. A second, improved pad—still based on the old model of menstruation, the model Tom believed was flawed—was even more successful. When his small test panel results were announced, some managers did not believe that Tom's prototype could provide sufficient absorption. Still others disregarded the data because they believed Tom's model of menstruation was inaccurate; therefore, his data must be flawed. Managers who were looking at the current business results had no reason or incentive to push for a major change to the current product.

Once again, Tom was forbidden from further work on the project. And again, he was headed for termination. This time, he solicited letters of support from his allies across the technical community. It was a struggle to convince the senior supervisor to read the letters, but he did and the termination process was delayed—"for right now."

Tom used his latest reprieve to continue validating the new model, developing the new product, and searching for potential allies at higher levels. This time, fortune was in his favor. Another new manager rotated into Tom's group. Like Tom, he was a chemist by training. He believed in Tom's model and data. The new manager approved another test for Tom's prototype, a head-to-head, large sample comparison against the organization's competing upgrade product. Again, Tom's pad was the undisputed winner. It was more comfortable and sufficiently absorbent, and estimated production costs for Tom's pad were far less than for the upgrade product. Yet key managers remained unconvinced. The already-commercialized products were huge market successes, having gained significant market share against already-entrenched incumbent products.

Once again, Tom leveraged his networking and relationship-building skills to gain internal product acceptance. Fortunately, P&G culture doesn't discourage lower-level employees from building relationships with managers. Tom had recently met the new director of the entire paper organization socially, and he reached out to him. The director said, "Make an appointment and tell me about it." Tom invited his direct managers to the meeting, but they declined. The new director, who was not invested in the old model or technology, found the data compelling. But given the success of the current products, he did not push Tom's model or product idea.

Shortly thereafter, Tom ran into a former colleague, now heading paper R&D at one of P&G's international R&D locations. He was interested in the new product, based on a belief that comfort was very important in his market, and ran new tests on Tom's prototypes in his geographic region. The results were stellar. Soon after, a feminine hygiene pad of Tom's design was launched abroad.

Despite the successful launch of feminine pads based on the old model, momentum had finally shifted to the thin-and-comfortable concept. With two important senior management Champions, the rest of the organization now rallied to the new model and product. The Always Ultra concept was fully supported, staffed, and globally launched. Women around the world experienced a radical and positive change in the way they dealt with their monthly periods. Now in its third decade, successive generations of

Always Ultra continue to deliver protection *and* comfort for women, as well as huge profits for P&G.

In 1998, Tom was inducted into the Victor Mills Society, the company's highest level of recognition for R&D leadership and creativity. Reflecting on the Always Ultra experience nearly a quarter of a century later, Tom notes that P&G—including managers who once opposed him—values diverse perspectives and different ways of framing problems. In fact, P&G now puts ongoing effort toward developing new approaches to innovation and nurturing many kinds of Innovators. He also believes that his Always Ultra experience helped him develop relationship and communication skills that have proven invaluable in all aspects of his career and life.

THE PROBLEMS WITH SERIAL INNOVATORS

The Always Ultra story is likely far more information about feminine hygiene issues and products than the readers of this book (whether male or female) ever wanted to know (and certainly more than coauthors Ray and Bruce ever wanted to know). But Tom's story exemplifies how a profitable product almost did not get developed because Serial Innovators work differently from other development people, reconceptualizing product categories and businesses and frequently breaking organizational rules and norms, all of which can lead to difficulty managing them successfully. Their innovation process is very different from the formal new product development (NPD) processes found in firms. It frequently starts with developing an understanding of the basic science behind a particular phenomena or problem and spending significant time personally understanding customer needs. Serial Innovators tend to take personal responsibility for gaining and maintaining the political acceptance for a project. Thus, "talent management" of these individuals must help them manage their innovation, development, and political navigation processes.

Tom's plight is not a singular one. In 1982, HP created and bestowed upon Chuck House the "Medal of Defiance" for successfully continuing development of one of his major innovations after being specifically told to cease and desist. Chuck also was demoted back to lower levels of the HP organization twice during his career. Ironically, he was relieved to be demoted; within the strictures of the organization, he was better able to innovate as a lower-level employee.

On the one hand, then, Serial Innovators are valuable members of an organization—perhaps the most valuable individuals in the firm, as they are capable of creating breakthrough innovations that capture large new revenue streams. On the other hand, they can be difficult to manage successfully in the context of the typical organizational innovation and NPD processes.

The purpose of this book is thus to help you understand

- how Serial Innovators differ from others involved in the development and innovation processes in the organization and the general model depicting how they understand problems and create solutions (Chapter 1);

- how Serial Innovators operate in the context of the organization, both in terms of their innovation "process" (Chapters 2 and 3) and in managing the politics of innovation (Chapter 4);

- what characteristics differentiate Serial Innovators from others in the organization in terms of personality, perspective, motivation, and preparation (Chapter 5);

- how the organization can identify and develop Serial Innovators (Chapter 6);

- how Serial Innovators are managed most effectively (Chapter 7); and

- our recommendations and challenges for those who are or who hope to become Serial Innovators, or those who would like to manage or work productively with them (Chapter 8).

Some of the chapters in the book, such as Chapters 1 (the general framework for understanding Serial Innovators in the context of NPD), 2 (their innovation process), 4 (how they manage the politics of the organization), and 5 (Serial Innovator characteristics), are purely descriptive and recount what we saw in our research. Their purpose is to help readers identify Serial Innovators and understand who they are and how they do what they do.

Other chapters move beyond the direct observations of our research, prescribing how to better manage Serial Innovators to maximize their probable success. Chapter 3, for example, describes a number of techniques

Serial Innovators use to uncover customer problems in detail. It also provides suggestions that will help managers support these workers in this very important task. Chapter 6 describes how to identify Serial Innovators and then suggests how to cultivate nascent Serial Innovators to realize their full potential. Finally, Chapter 7 is fully prescriptive. It contains all of our advice for successfully managing Serial Innovators. The book closes with Chapter 8, which directs "love letters" with advice individualized to each of the different constituencies targeted in the preface.

ABOUT THIS RESEARCH

This research has taken place across a number of phases over nearly a decade. Even though we all worked at the same university, this project began with two disjointed investigations. Unbeknownst to each other, Abbie had started investigating people she termed "Product Visionaries" about the same time Ray and Bruce started a project about people they termed "Technical Visionaries." Amazingly, the two groups were brought together by the director of an NSF branch whom we separately had approached to explore funding opportunities. We are eternally grateful that they put us in contact with each other.

The early research used the terms *Product* and *Technical Visionaries*. However, we found the word "Visionary" problematic. We were looking for people who were more than just visionary—we were trying to understand people who actually had developed multiple products and moved them through to market. Ultimately, we settled on "Serial Innovators" as the term that best described their entire range of finding and understanding problems, inventing, and bringing new solutions to the marketplace.

In the first research in this stream (Vojak et al. 2006), ten technology managers in high-tech industries were interviewed to define which characteristics most frequently appear in industrial Technical Visionaries. Industrial Technical Visionaries were defined as "technical individuals who effectively synthesize multiple technologies and business strategy to identify new and innovative breakthrough products and processes." Then, 418 American and British industrial physicists were surveyed to determine their perceptions of how important each of the characteristics was to the success of Technical Visionaries.

The next project investigated how Technical Visionaries are motivated and demotivated (Hebda et al. 2007; Hebda 2012), through structured in-depth interviews with twenty-four Technical Visionaries, their twenty-two technical managers, and their eighteen human resource managers. These individuals came from seventeen companies in the following industries: aerospace and defense; automotive and transport; chemicals; computer hardware; computer services; consumer products manufacturers; electronics; industrial manufacturing; medical equipment; and telecommunications equipment. Material from this research helped shape Chapters 6 and 7.

In 2002, *Electronic Design* celebrated its fiftieth year of publication. To mark this anniversary, they officially established an Engineering Hall of Fame, inducting fifty-eight individuals representing fifty landmark lifetime achievements. More than twenty-five thousand *Electronic Design* readers determined the honorees through online voting. We developed the general model describing Serial Innovators (described in Chapter 1 and Figure 1.6 in this book) from an in-depth investigation of how eleven of the thirty-three still-living inductees created their breakthrough innovations (Griffin et al. 2009).

Another project investigated three Serial Innovators, two Inventors, two Champions, and two Implementers in one large firm (Griffin et al. 2007). We conducted in-depth interviews with each of them, and with seventeen of their coworkers and managers, to understand what persons in each role do in organizations, and how they differ from each other in their methods, personalities, and attitudes. Chapter 1 is drawn in part from this project.

At that point, we finally embarked on "the big project," by interviewing additional Serial Innovators from a diverse set of industries that included: agribusiness, consumer packaged goods, electronics, engineering services, heavy manufacturing, medical devices, and paper products (Price et al. 2009). Some of these individuals were found through self-nomination or nomination by another in their firm after they listened to one of us present some of our findings at conferences. Others we found through our industry contacts. When someone was nominated, we first conducted a preinterview to determine whether they met our requirements of having driven at least two successful breakthrough products to market. In this process, we eliminated nearly half of those initially nominated. In addition to interviewing over thirty of their coworkers and managers, we interviewed most of these Serial Innovators multiple times, producing a very rich set of data.

In writing this book, we worked from the data generated across all our projects.

I BREAKTHROUGH INNOVATION IN MATURE FIRMS*

This chapter describes the

- Different types of innovations firms need to commercialize to both support their ongoing businesses and grow their firms into new market space;

- General processes by which both incremental and breakthrough innovations most typically are developed, and why creating successful breakthrough innovations is so difficult;

- Different tasks that people in various innovation roles perform;

- Positioning of the Serial Innovator model of innovation vis-à-vis the technology push and market pull models; and

- General structure and components of the MP^5 Model of Serial Innovators and how they innovate, which drives the structure of the rest of this book.

---

* As indicated in the "About This Research" section in the Introduction to the book, this research was conducted in large, mature, U.S. corporations. However, we believe that the contexts within which these findings apply are broader than just large for-profit firms. Government institutions such as NASA, NIH, and the Department of Defense's research labs all may house Serial Innovators, or individuals with the potential to become Serial Innovators. While some of their breakthrough products may not be targeted for or ever reach a civilian or for-profit marketplace (think "MREs" or meals ready to eat), others may in fact find commercial applications in addition to space or military ones (think memory or "Tempur® foam").

Firms need to support two types of innovation to stay competitive and in business. They need incremental innovation that provides ongoing improvements to current products and product lines.* However, they also need breakthrough or radical† innovation that produces enormous performance increases in current products (e.g., a fivefold or more increase in the performance of current features or at least a 30% decrease in cost to produce) or results in innovative products that move the firm into new white space by providing an entirely new set of performance features (Liefer et al. 2000). These two types of innovation need different development processes.

INNOVATING TO SUPPORT THE ONGOING BUSINESS

The majority of the firm's development efforts, over three-fourths of the total number of projects undertaken (Barczak et al. 2009), are spent improving the performance of products currently marketed or adding new products to current product lines. These projects tend to improve or change product performance incrementally.

Typical product improvement efforts for a diesel engine manufacturer might be a new engine with increased fuel efficiency or decreased emissions. Other examples of product improvements include faster computer chips, smaller and lighter laptops, easier to operate software, softer bread, and creamier ice cream. While significant engineering or development effort may be required to achieve these goals, the desired outcomes are rather predictable and to consumers appear evolutionary in nature. These projects are necessary to retain customers over time, providing them with reasons to repurchase from your firm, rather than from your competitors. Firms that do not continue to renew and improve their current products stagnate and lose customers to competitors. The U.S. car industry's failure to evolve and to upgrade their small car offerings has contributed significantly to their demise, as Kia, Hyundai, and even BMW (Mini) and

---

* The term *products* refers throughout the book to physical goods, services, combinations of physical goods and services, processes, and software. The Serial Innovators we studied worked in all of these areas.
† For simplicity and consistency, we refer to these types of innovations as "breakthrough innovations" for the remainder of the book, following O'Connor et al. (2008).

Smart have materially encroached into this segment of the U.S. and global automobile market.

Developing products that expand a current product line allows firms to increase usage with current customers. For consumers who value variety, larger product lines may mean increased absolute consumption. If, for example, Abbie kept only two varieties of granola bars in the pantry, her son might have a granola bar for a snack after school two or three days a week, substituting some other snack on the other days. However, if the cupboard held six or seven different granola bar flavors, he might choose granola bars as his after-school snack four or five days a week, increasing his absolute consumption of granola bars, at the expense of another snack food. Variety-seeking is a major reason why grocery stores have one full aisle of ready-to-eat cereal, and why some closets contain forty to fifty pairs of shoes.

Extending a current product line also may attract new customers, whose tastes or needs differ somewhat from those satisfied by current offerings. When yogurt manufacturers expanded from fruit-flavored yogurts to chocolate flavors, their targets were chocoholics who previously had not been yogurt consumers because they were not fruit fans. Similarly, the primary users of Palm's PDAs traditionally were professionals until the company's Zire line extension specifically targeted the broader market of students and nonprofessionals. While the Zire used the same operating system and had a similar look and feel, it was less expensive than the professional Palm and was differentiated from the rest of the line by simplicity: it had a monochrome screen without backlighting, only two quick buttons instead of four, and a traditional up/down navigation button instead of a five-way navigator.

Developing line extensions involves slightly greater effort and risk than developing incremental improvements to current products. Such changes require more research into customer needs, for example. Even still, the development effort is predominantly evolutionary and predictable. Given this predictability, the probability of success can be maximized by implementing formal product development processes. Indeed, over the last twenty-five years, academics and practitioners have made great strides in understanding how to manage these projects more effectively and efficiently, and in

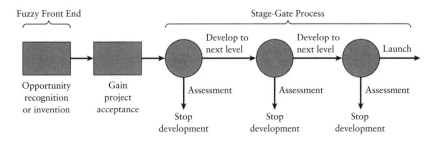

FIGURE I.I   A typical Stage-Gate new product development process
Source: Vojak et al. (2010). Reprinted by permission of Oxford University Press.

developing formal processes for doing so. These formal processes, such as the Stage-Gate® process illustrated in Figure 1.1, ensure that none of the details necessary for successful development are overlooked, specify who is responsible for completing which tasks, and provide a road map for when various milestones should be achieved. Currently, the majority of companies have implemented some sort of formal new product development (NPD) process, allowing them to commercialize successful product improvements and line extensions more routinely (Barczak et al. 2009).

MOVING FIRMS INTO NEW COMPETITIVE SPACE

Fewer than one-fourth of the firm's innovation projects focus on goods and services that will move the firm into new competitive space. Most of those projects (60% of the 25%, or 15% of all of the projects a firm undertakes) are products that another firm already has commercialized. For example, should Ford Motor Company develop a theme park featuring cars and automotive history, this type of product would move the company into new market space. However, the product is one that other firms, notably Disney, already have developed. Thus, while this development is more risky for Ford than creating a next-generation improvement to one of their current car models, there are examples in the market that Ford could use as templates to reduce its commercialization risk.

The other 40% of projects that will move a firm into new market space (approximately 10% of all of the projects the firm undertakes) are concepts that are "new-to-the-world." They are breakthrough products for which there are no competitors already in the market. The original PalmPilot®,

HP's logic analyzer, and Mrs. Dash® all are examples of breakthrough products. Firms have no starting template from which to create these products and bring them to market; these projects require overcoming high market and technical unknowns, uncertainties, and risks.

CREATING BREAKTHROUGH INNOVATION

The typical Stage-Gate process, which works so well for incremental innovation where there are few market or technical uncertainties, does not work well for creating breakthrough products. These processes are deficient in two ways. First, the formal NPD processes used in firms assume that the product is conceptualized already and that the technology development is more or less complete. Second, they assume that projects have been approved and accepted by management for development. Stage-Gate types of processes are not helpful in navigating through the "Fuzzy Front End" (FFE) of innovation or in obtaining initial corporate approval and funding for a project. Formal innovation processes are applicable only once technical invention is demonstrated and the project is accepted by the firm for development (Figure 1.1).

The FFE is the "messy, getting started" phase of product development (Smith and Reinertsen 1992). In the FFE, customer problems are understood in great depth, potential solutions to those problems are conceived, and the technologies necessary to turn those potential solutions into concrete products are found or invented. Incremental innovations have little or no FFE. Project teams are executing product improvements against well-known customer needs. For line extensions, only a minimal amount of effort is needed to understand customer needs, which is easily incorporated into the beginning of the formal development process. Even for products that are new to the firm, but already are commercialized by others, the FFE is fairly easy to complete by drawing on extant knowledge about the competitors' products and the customers and markets served.

The FFE requires expending a significant effort for breakthrough innovation projects because the firm is entering unknown markets and technologies. Creating breakthrough products requires an in-depth understanding of a broad (and most likely complex) set of unsolved problems for some target market—and perhaps for a target market for which the firm has

FIGURE 1.2   "Connecting Customer Needs with Technology Solutions"
Source: © Sidney Harris (2010), reprinted with permission.

little extant knowledge. Then, somehow, those needs must be connected to some potential solution, which then must be invented in a process that frequently is reminiscent of the cartoon in Figure 1.2.

No formal process has been developed to help innovation teams routinely and successfully navigate the FFE for breakthrough innovation projects. Indeed, some suggest that the term *processes* is not appropriate for describing what happens in the FFE because "process" denotes structure, whereas the FFE is inherently chaotic and nonlinear (Koen et al. 2002). Indeed, a multicompany project team investigating this issue, consisting of members of the Industrial Research Institute and facilitated by an academic researcher, has proposed a circular "engine" for managing the FFE, with ideas flowing, circulating, and iterating across five elements: opportunity identification, opportunity analysis, idea generation and enrichment, idea selection, and concept selection (http://www.iriweb .org/). This FFE engine starts with opportunity identification—locating a new market or technology arena the firm wants to enter—which is driven by the firm's business goals.

Breakthrough projects frequently are initiated as "technology push" endeavors. That is, they start out in the firm's research and development (R&D) laboratory. Creating significant breakthrough products from technology push initiatives is very difficult. Only half (six of twelve) of the technology push inventions studied for over a decade by the Rensselaer Radical Innovation Project resulted in a new product commercialized from the technology developed (Liefer et al. 2000). Additionally, many of the products that were commercialized did not result in the significant revenue and profit stream for the firm that was expected at their initiation.

In a similar pattern, Michael Valocchi, head of IBM's Smarter Planet Research Initiative, expects that only about half of the initiative's FOAK, or "first of a kind," projects will result in a commercially developed product for the company—even though IBM is developing new capabilities that are targeted to particular, well-recognized global problems (e.g., how to quickly pinpoint where an outage has originated on a utility's electrical grid). IBM invested $1.8 billion in this type of long-term research in 2009, with fifty smart-grid research projects under way (O'Brien 2009).

In other words, even for companies that are very good at inventing new technologies, achieving commercial success from those technologies can be difficult. Firms frequently fail in commercializing breakthrough innovations based on technology push strategies for two very different reasons.

First, many technology push initiatives produce "a hammer that is looking for a nail"—a technology that does not provide any immediate profit for the company because no viable commercial applications have been identified. Typical of these projects is the DuPont Biomax® story (for a more complete recounting, see Liefer et al. 2000, 12–16). In the late 1980s, DuPont's executives commanded the scientists in their R&D laboratories to "invent their way out" of the company's financial woes. As a result, one of the materials invented in 1989 was Biomax, a "biodegradable" polyester-based material that would function as designed for some specified period of time and conditions, and then would decompose and could be recycled. By 1992, with no sales, "Biomax seemed destined to sit on the shelf—one of many good ideas developed by DuPont scientists for which no market application could be found" (Liefer et al. 2000, 14). Over the next four years, business development managers still were unable to find commercial applications for this material, but the company persisted, believing that the invention was still potentially valuable. Biomax products still can be purchased from DuPont (http://www2.dupont.com/ Biomax/en_US/); however, the initially expected large sales volumes and high returns have never materialized. The financial benefits of this project have been incommensurate with the investment.

Second, many breakthrough innovations that originate out of the technology organization do not get commercialized because they cannot cross the so-called "Valley of Death" (Markham 2002). The Valley of Death is the gap between the firm's personnel and organizational structures that are in place for technology development, and those resources and structures that are in place for commercialization activities. Commercialization resources include marketing, sales promotion, production, and distribution. Because the resources necessary for commercializing new products differ from those technical resources needed for inventing new technologies, and because they are disconnected from those resources, even the most important breakthrough inventions may fall into the Valley of Death and fail to be commercialized.

Although many breakthrough innovations start out as technology push endeavors, some breakthrough products are market-driven in their origin. Pert Plus® is one such example. As women flocked to the workforce in the 1970s, Procter & Gamble's (P&G) marketing people heard over and over again that there was a need for a shampoo that both cleaned hair and simultaneously conditioned it. A "2-in-1" hair product would decrease the number of bottles that had to be packed for travel or use at the gym, and decrease the overall amount of time needed for hair washing/conditioning. In this case, the market needs were well defined, but the technical goal was difficult to achieve. Overall, it took ten years to invent the technology; the project was pursued diligently for a period of time, was shelved as one or another technical pathway failed, and was pursued again later by other technologists who were inspired to tackle the problem. Finally, technical success was achieved by radically changing the surfactant system from the usual anionic system in shampoos and conditioners to a silicone-based system. Pert Plus, the resulting product, was an immediate market success and is still creating profits for the company decades later in the very competitive shampoo category. Thus, while technology push endeavors may fail because the invention either does not sufficiently solve an important customer or market problem or because there is no organizational structure or mechanism in place to move it from the technology group into acceptance for development, market-driven breakthrough innovation endeavors may fail because there just is no technology that can solve that particular problem. Wouldn't you just love to avoid traveling by airplane by being materialized from one point to another, à la "Beam me up, Scotty," in *Star Trek*?

In summary, breakthrough products that are potentially important to a firm can originate using either a technology push or market-driven endeavor. Both types of endeavor are essential for long-term success. However, creating successful breakthrough products is difficult, independent of whether the process begins as a technology push or as market-need-driven. We do not always have the requisite technologies available to solve a particular problem. Inventing technical solutions that actually solve a problem can be prohibitively time-consuming, if those solutions can be found at all. On the other hand, it can be similarly difficult to identify a significant problem that a particular technology solves after the fact. There is no standard process for achieving the most important tasks needed to complete the FFE—to match good technical solutions to problems that are significant and important to potential customers. Creating breakthrough products can be even more difficult in large, mature firms because of the specialization of labor into the different tasks of innovation and development, as seen in the Valley of Death problem.

WHO DEVELOPS NEW PRODUCTS IN FIRMS

A number of major tasks must be completed to generate breakthrough products: needs finding and understanding, invention, project acceptance, and project implementation or facilitation. Finding and understanding needs takes place in the FFE, as does invention. Gaining project acceptance requires developing a business plan for the proposed product or service and shepherding that plan through the firm's funding and staffing process. This task fundamentally requires managing the politics of gaining project acceptance in the firm. Once the project is accepted by the organization, getting the product to market is a matter of project execution and implementation.

Needs understanding, technology invention, project definition and acceptance, and process execution each require different competencies to

TABLE I.I   Innovation skills and traditional roles

Core skills	Inventor	Champion	Implementer
Technical	**Primary**	Secondary	Secondary
Market insight		**Primary**	
"Political" savvy		**Primary**	
Project facilitation			**Primary**

complete successfully (Schumpeter 1934). Invention in the FFE requires technical competency and creativity. Needs understanding involves developing business, market, and customer knowledge, and applying the tools of marketing research. Project acceptance requires business, market, and some technical knowledge, coupled with a driving political capability. Project implementation depends upon project management and facilitation skills. In a traditional NPD setting found in large firms, individuals with different skills undertake the various roles involved with moving an innovation opportunity through the laboratory, gaining political acceptance for it as a project, and managing the formal commercialization process. These individuals have complementary skill sets, as shown in Table 1.1. In the classical view of NPD, because of the different skills required, the three breakthrough innovation stages (the FFE, project acceptance, and product implementation) are most frequently driven or managed by Inventor technologists, Champions, and Implementers, respectively (Figure 1.3).

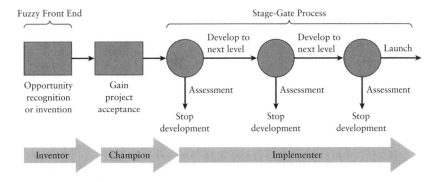

FIGURE I.3   Innovation roles
Source: Vojak et al. (2010). Reprinted by permission of Oxford University Press.

Inventor technologists tend to be the originators of innovative capabilities and ideas in the FFE (Maidique 1980; Rice et al. 2001). An Inventor creates a technical capability that can be used to create products or features that solve a customer problem or market need. Industrial Inventors focus on improving, transforming, or creating technologies.

A Champion recognizes a new technology or market opportunity as having significant potential, adopts the project as his or her own, and takes a passionate interest in seeing that a particular product is fully developed and marketed, using any and every means of informal tactics and pressure to make it succeed (Markham and Aiman-Smith 2001). Champions typically are not technologists who can create innovative ideas, but they have the business and marketing savvy to find technologies created by the organization and understand those technologies' potential. Champions are not formally assigned to projects, but arise informally. They are the necessary ingredient in moving technology push projects across the Valley of Death and into commercialization (Markham 2002).

Product implementation is managed by a project manager who is assigned formally to the project. He or she is responsible for organizing the execution of the project once it reaches the firm's formal NPD process and for ensuring that each task and milestone is completed on time and within budget. Project managers have excellent facilitation skills. While they frequently are technologists, they do not have the sophisticated technical skills of Inventors.

Interestingly, in most organizations, there is a responsibility void in performing the tasks necessary for creating successful breakthrough innovations. As the Rensselaer Polytechnic Institute (RPI) Radical Innovation Project found, the Inventors creating the technical and scientific breakthroughs in firms' R&D labs had little or no business or market research training; they were hired because they had strong technical and scientific skills (Liefer et al. 2000; O'Connor et al. 2008). They were not responsible for creating needs understanding, which typically is the responsibility of the marketing or marketing research function. However, the firm's marketing functions do not participate in the FFE of the breakthrough innovation process. They typically only become involved much later in the project, during implementation. In some cases, the Champion has enough marketing savvy to help with needs understanding. In general, however, by the time the Champion is involved, invention is mostly complete, and the Champion's job is just to identify an appropriate market application for the technology.

Thus, Inventors, Champions, and Implementers each manage different aspects of breakthrough innovation, and no individual is responsible for generating needs understanding in the FFE to support generating break-through innovation. Indeed, this situation is precisely what leads to break-through innovations that are "hammers looking for nails."

Not all projects may require all three types of individuals. For example, Inventors may not be needed for incremental projects where there is no significant new "invention," or when a team is simply asked to develop to a specific product specification change or performance improvement. The project implementation team in those cases frequently has the development capability necessary to move performance forward slightly, or to change or add flavors, for example. In projects where there is high technical uncertainty but low customer or market uncertainty, as with the case of Pert Plus, when there was a well-known problem in the marketplace but no sufficient product solution, a Champion may not be necessary to obtain project acceptance. In this case, both technologists and product managers at P&G "knew" for many years that there was an unfilled need for a combination shampoo and conditioner. Thus, while the Inventor was required to develop a solution, a Champion for the project was not needed. Management sat poised to commercialize the product—if it could only be invented.

The general picture of innovation that emerges is one of different types of people, with complementary knowledge bases and skill sets, who tend to perform various (and often disjointed) tasks across the overall innovation process. In this prevailing model, there is a needs understanding skills gap in the FFE.

However, in every firm we have studied, we also have found individuals, who we describe as "Innovators," who perform all four tasks: they understand needs and invent, champion, and facilitate projects through the implementation process (Figure 1.4). And they innovate over and over again. We refer to individuals who use these skills to create multiple

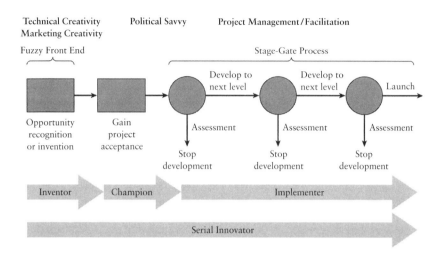

FIGURE 1.4   Innovator roles
Source: Vojak et al. (2010). Reprinted by permission of Oxford University Press.

breakthrough products during their career as "Serial Innovators." While rare—research suggests that they constitute between one in fifty and one in two hundred of a firm's professional technical staff (Vojak et al. 2006)—Serial Innovators are important to understand because they have the potential to create significant revenue and profit streams for an organization over the course of their careers.

As Table 1.2 shows, Innovators have the combined skill sets of Inventors, Champions, Implementers, *and* market researchers. Because of their combination of skill sets, they overcome a major problem when trying to create breakthrough products using a traditional organizational structure (O'Connor et al. 2008). In traditional technology push breakthrough innovation, the scientists who invent technical solutions have little or no knowledge of business, markets, or customer problems. As marketers and market researchers generally are not involved in the FFE, there are no other mechanisms for generating customer needs understanding in that phase. Because of their skill sets, Innovators fill these marketing and customer needs understanding voids. Their methods for understanding customer needs are so important to the success of breakthrough innovation that we discuss these methods in depth in Chapter 3.

TABLE 1.2   Innovation skills and expanded roles

Core skills	Inventor	Champion	Implementer	Innovator
Technical	**Primary**	Secondary	Secondary	**Primary**
Market insight		**Primary**		**Primary**
"Political" savvy		**Primary**		**Primary**
Project facilitation			**Primary**	Secondary

A THIRD PATHWAY TO GENERATING BREAKTHROUGH INNOVATION: INNOVATOR-DRIVEN

The RPI research on technology push breakthrough innovation (Liefer et al. 2000; O'Connor et al. 2008) predominantly takes the perspective that there is a temporal directionality in the tasks that are undertaken:

- Discovery (creation, recognition, elaboration, and articulation of opportunities) occurs first. This phase uses basic research to identify new concepts, or hunts for them internally or externally.

- Incubation, which occurs after discovery, evolves the idea or concept into a business proposition. Technical and market learning and market creation occur at this stage.

- Acceleration then focuses investment to stimulate growth, building the business rapidly to a point of maturity where it can survive as part of the mainstream company.

Another important point from this research is that "someone"—an innovation board or a chief innovation officer—is needed to manage projects across the interfaces of the three blocks of breakthrough innovation. Their findings echo Markham (2002): technology push projects need Champions to manage them across the Valley of Death.

Market pull projects also assume a temporal directionality. In this orientation, however, the firm starts from understanding market needs and then tries to find a technology to solve the customer problems. In these cases, while the general customer problems are transmitted to the technologists from the marketing group ("a better feminine hygiene pad"), the details of what that means may not get transmitted (e.g., "captures fluid completely"; "is comfortable to wear"; "is invisible to those around the wearer"; etc.). Again, the technologists generally do not have the capability to generate that needs understanding themselves. Not understanding the details makes creating that breakthrough innovation more difficult.

The Innovator-driven breakthrough process is neither technology push nor market pull, but an integrative combination of the two, as shown in Figure 1.5. Serial Innovators alternate repeatedly between generating micro-level customer understanding and seeking potential technology solutions, while making occasional forays into the market overall to generate macro-level market knowledge and to determine whether the problem/solution under investigation is potentially interesting to the market in aggregate. This book is not meant to disparage either technology push or market pull breakthrough innovation endeavors. Both approaches have led, and will continue to lead, to important and world-changing new products. Rather, this book shows readers a third mechanism—Innovator-driven innovation—by which firms can develop breakthrough new products. Further, we describe the characteristics and the processes of the Serial

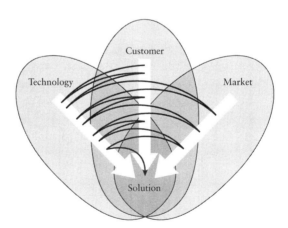

FIGURE 1.5   The convergence of generating customer and technology
              understanding
Source: Griffin et al. (2009). Reprinted by permission from the *Journal of Product
Innovation Management*.

Innovators who generate these breakthrough innovations, offer ways to help managers harness the potential of these rare employees, and seek to help aspiring Serial Innovators learn how to innovate.

The last section of this chapter provides a brief overview introducing each of the six elements of the Serial Innovator model. The remainder of the book is organized around these elements and provides detailed information about them.

HOW SERIAL INNOVATORS IN LARGE, MATURE ORGANIZATIONS INNOVATE: THE MP^5 MODEL

Figure 1.6 describes the general characteristics and behaviors that epitomize Serial Innovators and differentiate them from other researchers and managers in mature firms. The four dimensions of the model inside the

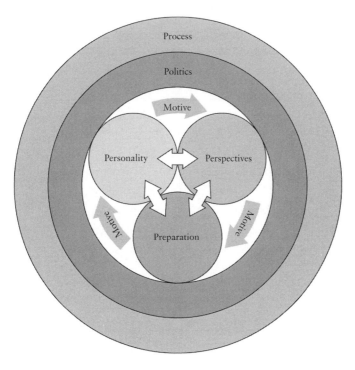

FIGURE 1.6   The MP^5 Model of Serial Innovators
Source: Griffin et al. (2009). Reprinted by permission from the *Journal of Product Innovation Management*.

circles represent the Serial Innovator's individual characteristics and capabilities. Serial Innovators are encircled by how they must apply these
capabilities within the confines and constraints of the organization; they
must also develop processes and political capabilities that allow them to
work effectively with others in the organization to develop, gain acceptance for, and commercialize breakthrough products. Managing Serial
Innovators requires understanding who they are, how they innovate, and
why they are driven to do so.

The three elements in the interior circles in Figure 1.6 are factors that
derive from the individual's past. They predominantly arise independent of
the firm, but are important in defining what distinguishes Serial Innovators
from other employees. Serial Innovators bring these characteristics into
the firm fully (or at least partially) formed. Understanding an individual's
personality and perspective or worldview, which are fully formed when
they join the organization, may allow a firm to identify individuals in the
organization early in their careers who may have the potential to become
Serial Innovators in the future.

Serial Innovators also bring to the organization a significant level of
technical training or preparation. However, this technical training is not
sufficient to allow them to create breakthrough innovations; it is only sufficient to allow them to invent new technical solutions to difficult problems.
Thus, at some point during their working careers, they also must obtain
additional knowledge and/or training about business, strategy, and marketing to ensure that the inventing they undertake will prove valuable to
some set of potential purchasers and concomitantly to the firm.

Their newly developed business savvy then combines with their innate
individual characteristics (personality and perspective) to drive (motivate)
them to develop both the processes and political capabilities they need to
create breakthrough products within the organizational structures and
constraints of the firm. As the firm's formal product development processes typically are insufficient to support breakthrough innovation, potential Serial Innovators must develop additional process capabilities over
and above those already resident in the firm that nonetheless are compatible with existing processes. Finally, because Serial Innovators are always
competing with other projects and initiatives for resources, they also must

learn how to influence the firm to accept their projects. The remainder of this chapter briefly introduces each aspect of process, politics, personality, perspective, motivation, and preparation—the MP⁵ Model.

These Serial Innovators generally have strong **Personalities** with several distinct characteristics that contribute to how they creatively think and behave. Personality, the way a person is hardwired, is relatively difficult to change. It generally coalesces long before an individual enters the workforce. While many of the typical personality traits of highly creative people were revealed, such as an innate curiosity and a high tolerance for ambiguity, one of the Serial Innovator's defining personality characteristics is that they are "systems thinkers." For them, the whole is much more than just the sum of the parts. They do not think about the features of a product individually, rather they consider the entire functioning of a product. In addition to these defining characteristics, which support their inventive capability, Serial Innovators also have a number of personality characteristics that support their ability to stay deeply involved with a task over a long period of time.

Several specific **Perspectives**, or strongly held attitudes that add up to an overall worldview, of these Serial Innovators came out in our research. Their perspective on life tends to be simultaneously business-oriented and idealistic. On the one hand, nearly all the Serial Innovators voiced a belief that new products must be salable and profitable. Technology, while important, is just a means to an end—it keeps a business self-sustainable by creating profits. On the other hand, these Serial Innovators also voiced strong ethical attitudes. As one Serial Innovator put it, he "feels a moral responsibility to do the best he can." So, combining these two general perspectives, Serial Innovators want to use technology to solve people's problems and to make the world a better place, while making money for the company. Again, these worldviews have developed during their maturation to adulthood, so the Serial Innovator typically brings these attitudes to the workplace mostly formed.

Virtually every model of creativity includes intrinsic **Motivation** as one element of the framework (Amabile 1988; Lovelace 1986). It is not surprising, then, that another individual element in our model of Serial Innovators is their high motivation to create. However, rather than just being intrinsically motivated to be creative, their motivation is *directed*. It consists of two forces. First, customers and firms with urgent and important problems are a powerful external force that motivates Serial Innovators. This force works in concert with an acute intrinsic desire to tackle unsolved problems, and the personal satisfaction the Serial Innovators derive when they do solve such problems. Thus, it is a strong and interacting combination of external and internal forces that motivates these Serial Innovators.

Each Serial Innovator takes specific steps during their formative years to **Prepare** themselves for innovating, and they continue learning and expanding the domains of their knowledge throughout their careers. They are lifelong learners. Their preparation activities take place across multiple domains, including obtaining technical, business, and market understanding. These Serial Innovators have worked to develop great depth in their own fields; each also has sought out education in technology domains peripheral to their field of core competence. They learn what others in both their specializations and in neighboring fields are doing or attempting with technology. Business understanding is only infrequently acquired through formal mechanisms such as pursuing an MBA, but much more often through individual informal initiatives or with the help of a mentor.

While the previous four dimensions of the model are about the Serial Innovator and his or her personal capabilities, the two dimensions in the outer rings of the model of Figure 1.6 represent how the Serial Innovator operates in the context of an organization. Successful Serial Innovators have developed both a process that increases their probability of creating breakthrough innovations and a political capability that enables them to obtain project acceptance and the necessary organizational resources to take the product to market. These two dimensions represent how Serial Innovators operate in the present.

The **Process** used by these Serial Innovators has three unique aspects compared to the Stage-Gate types of processes in the product development literature. First, their processes are highly dynamic across domains, with Serial Innovators iterating across the customer, technology, and market throughout the entire process, as shown in Figure 1.5. Serial Innovators start by trying to find a bona fide customer problem. Then they immerse themselves in the technology domains and work to obtain a very broad understanding of why this is a problem and why it has not been solved before, iterating back and forth between technology and customer as needed to obtain a full understanding. At various points, information is taken back to the broader market and checked for validity, to determine whether other potential customers who could benefit from a specific innovation might constitute a market that would be large enough to be interesting to the firm. There is nearly continuous interplay between technical development and obtaining customer information and feedback, with periodic forays into the broader market to check for validity or generalizability of the solution.

Second, Serial Innovators' processes are nonlinear, with much more overlap, iteration, and feedback (Figure 1.7) than is found in a firm's typical linear product development process. They focus their initial attention on the top half of Figure 1.7, finding the right problem and understanding it deeply in order to create. Serial Innovators take specific actions in these early phases that are critical to breakthrough NPD, and that are very different from the "black box" view normally associated with the FFE.

Third, the processes Serial Innovators describe also are more far-reaching than the typical product development process on the

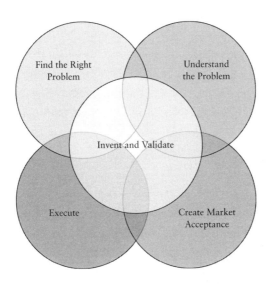

FIGURE 1.7   Innovation process used by Serial Innovators

post-commercialization side. Serial Innovators are absolutely committed to seeing their breakthrough products make it into the marketplace. They want to know what customers think of the product, how they use the product, and what should be done next. Further, they cite specific examples of how their products are affecting people's lives.

Just as important, the specific execution steps of physical development were seldom mentioned during interviews. Implementation followed the rather well-understood, generic, formal NPD process in place in the firm. Serial Innovators dwelled on aspects outside that standard execution process.

Unlike other highly creative individuals studied previously in great depth, Serial Innovators operate in the context of an organization. These Serial Innovators tend to work at the middle level of their organizations, whereas the previous literature has focused on individuals creating independently outside of an organizational context. Serial Innovators do not have a power position that would force acceptance of their projects. Consequently, they must develop the ability to successfully interact within their organizational environment; they must manage the **Politics** of the organization to successfully gain acceptance for the customer problems they solve. They know that they must sell their ideas to others, and that they have to work the political issues up (to management), laterally (with others needed to do the job), and externally (with customers and others whose expertise is needed). They depend upon influencing others to gain acceptance and resources. Generally, they focus on positive influencing actions, rather than coercion or other negative mechanisms. This political understanding enables these Serial Innovators to transfer interesting ideas and creative concepts into the implementation-focused commercialization process.

SUMMARY

As Figure 1.6 indicates, the Serial Innovator is surrounded by the need to develop and use two sets of organizational capabilities: a process that supports creating the breakthrough innovation and a political capability that lets him or her manage the organization. Chapters 2 and 3 elaborate on the details of the Serial Innovator's process. Chapter 4 describes in detail how Serial Innovators maneuver through the politics of the organization to gain acceptance for their projects.

As the arrows in Figure 1.6 suggest, the four individually related elements seem to interact in a mutually reinforcing manner. For example, aspects of their personalities likely have contributed to (or at least reinforce) their idealistic worldviews. Their perspective that people should try to improve the world drives them to identify important problems to solve and, in turn, contributes to their need to create useful products that help people. Their need to create pushes them to make the preparatory effort that enables developing new knowledge and seeing its application. These qualities result in a "whole individual" who can recognize important problems, has the personality and motivation to take them on, and has the knowledge underpinning to actually make a useful contribution.

Chapter 5 describes in depth the makeup of Serial Innovators: their personalities, perspectives, motivations, and how they prepare to innovate. Chapter 5 thus provides insight into some of the attributes and attitudes that can help managers identify potential Serial Innovators early in their careers and work to develop them, as we discuss further in Chapter 6. Chapter 7 discusses how the management of these Innovators should differ from other conventional management techniques.

We close the book with Chapter 8, which contains "love letters" to Serial Innovators, aspiring Serial Innovators, and all of those who work with and for them. These letters are meant to encourage, challenge, and warn each group concerning what they will face as participants in Innovator-driven breakthrough NPD.

THE PROCESSES BY WHICH
SERIAL INNOVATORS INNOVATE

Academic research on new product development (NPD) over the last several decades has taken the perspective that NPD could be managed and improved like any other complex process. Assuming that standard methods and protocols could be put into place that would result in an ongoing stream of successful new products, the field has worked to change the "art" of NPD to the "science" or process of NPD.

The NPD process most frequently used by firms is some variation of the generalized Stage-Gate® process (Cooper 1996) shown on the right-hand side of Figure 1.1. NPD efforts supporting ongoing businesses and product lines have well-defined objectives and high certainty in achieving those objectives, and these formal NPD processes have improved development efficiency and effectiveness (Barczak et al. 2009). However, the breakthrough innovations that Serial Innovators create do not start with already-developed concepts, and there are significant market and technical unknowns. Consequently, Stage-Gate processes are not particularly helpful to Serial Innovators as they create breakthrough innovations. Yes, Serial Innovators employ some of the Stage-Gate concepts in development—but only very late in the project.

Breakthrough innovations are different. The results are different. And the processes used to get those results must therefore be different. Serial

Innovators need more than just the firm's formal NPD process to create breakthrough products. Serial Innovators need a methodology that will allow them to find, understand, and invent to solve important customer problems—a method that allows them to "defuzz" the Fuzzy Front End (FFE) for a breakthrough innovation project.

We found that Serial Innovators' processes reflect some of the ideas that Koen et al. (2002) have presented. However, the Serial Innovators' FFE "process" is nonlinear and iterative, rather than just circular. At times, their process includes feedback loops from development back into the FFE, as they may have to go back and change their approach to solving a problem or change the problem on which they are working. Instead of the linear process for breakthrough innovation described elsewhere in literature on NPD, we observe a recurring pattern of nonlinearity and circularity in the FFE and also across the entire endeavor.

Figure 2.1 presents the overall hourglass "model" of how Serial Innovators develop new products. We developed this model from the stories our Serial Innovators told us about how they created their breakthrough innovations. Note that we are reluctant to use the words "process" and "stages" to describe Serial Innovators' activities or tasks, as these words imply a linearity that does not adequately represent the complexity of these innovation scenarios.

While the hourglass innovation model incorporates the firm's formal NPD process (as shown in the "Execute" circle), it also consists of three significant tasks of the FFE that must be completed prior to execution, and another task that Serial Innovators complete concurrently with—and after going through—the firm's formal process. Serial Innovators must visit each of the five tasks of Figure 2.1 at least once. However, they also may come back to each of the tasks multiple times, as needed, based on what they discover later in the project. We found that none of the Serial Innovators moved through the model in exactly the same way; they all took somewhat different paths, and each individual even took a different pathway through the model for different breakthrough innovations. However, in order to get to the overall goal—a breakthrough innovation that is launched flawlessly—they each had to complete all five of the main activities in the model.

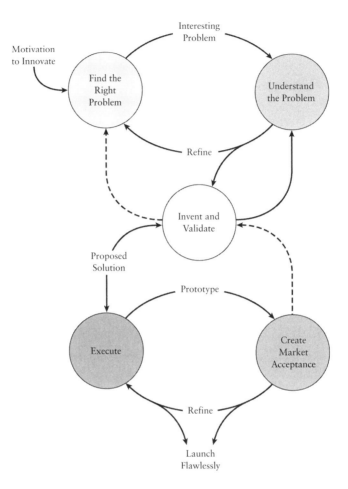

FIGURE 2.1   The hourglass model of Serial Innovators' NPD process
Source: Vojak et al. (2010). Reprinted by permission of Oxford University Press.

This chapter initially describes the general flow across the different tasks in the hourglass model, and then explores each of these tasks further in separate subsections. Chapter 3 delves deeply into how Serial Innovators engage potential customers throughout their innovation processes—a major differentiator in how Serial Innovators proceed in innovating, and one that is paramount to their success.

THE SERIAL INNOVATOR'S "HOURGLASS"
INNOVATION MODEL

Serial Innovators are intrinsically motivated to innovate—to develop solutions to really important customer problems and to ensure that those products get to market (Hebda et al. 2007). As we explain in Chapter 5, they are just built this way—a bit altruistic, but also motivated by profit. Because of this intrinsic motivation, Serial Innovators are driven to find interesting problems and to understand them completely. They spend a significant amount of time refining their understanding of interesting problems through a deep and broad application of fundamental principles. Slowly, after months or even years, their objectives shift from finding and understanding problems to inventing solutions. This shift marks a significant forward progression, moving them into the "second tier" of invention and validation. Like an hourglass, this second tier represents a checkpoint before, and sometimes a bottleneck within, the flow to commercialization. These three tasks comprise the Serial Innovator's FFE.

After they believe they have developed an appropriate and feasible solution to the right problem, they drop into the "third tier" of executable tasks. Here, a Serial Innovator circles between developing their solution as a sellable product using the firm's standard formal NPD processes and working to create market acceptance for that product. New learning in this third tier may necessitate another round of invention and validation. Both execution and market acceptance objectives feed into a flawless product launch, the end goal of the Serial Innovator's efforts. Notice that a flawless launch may not always translate into a marketplace success.

In Figure 2.1, the solid lines represent frequently taken pathways. The dotted lines are feedback loops taken with lower frequencies than the solid-line paths. While Serial Innovators circle repeatedly between developing products and creating market acceptance for them, they only rarely move back to reinventing and validating based on the feedback they get as they create market acceptance.

This model differs in three major ways from predominant depictions of product development. First, Serial Innovators approach product development nonlinearly. For example, they initially hover, circling between finding the right problem and taking steps to understand it, until they have enough information to move forward. They also circle repeatedly between developing the product and creating market acceptance. Second, Serial Innovators focus their energies on the FFE, rather than on execution. They spend a significant amount of time finding the "right" problem. They then also take time ensuring that they understand the problem completely. Serial Innovators may spend many months in their circular and extensive FFE before they have a concept that is developed sufficiently to enter into the firm's formal NPD process. During that time, they can appear highly unproductive, as little visible physical output may be generated.

Finally, Serial Innovators personally take steps to create market acceptance. Conventionally, this step is seen as the responsibility of marketing and sales, and if the sales force does not understand a product's ramifications or potential—as can frequently be the case with breakthrough innovations—they are less likely to push the product adequately or to educate potential customers as to its utility. Serial Innovators thus become acolytes for the product, helping both the sales force and customers to understand its potential.

Given these differences in how Serial Innovators approach innovation, managing them can be tricky. Somehow they have to be shielded from being pressed by management into shoving something—anything—into physical development before they are ready. We provide insights and advice into how to manage them most effectively in Chapter 7. Additionally, they have to be given both the money and, more important, the "permission" to make numerous forays into the field to engage potential customers all throughout the process. We provide insights about how they engage customers in Chapter 3 and advice for how to support them in accomplishing these tasks.

The remainder of this chapter elaborates on each of the tasks in the hourglass innovation model.

FINDING THE RIGHT PROBLEM

It takes as much time to solve a bad problem as it does a good problem. And if you're not working on good problems, you're really wasting your time.

Every Serial Innovator stressed the importance of finding the right problem to solve—what they call an "interesting" problem. Fascinatingly, they never use the word "opportunity" or the phrase "opportunity recognition." They are not looking for opportunities. They look for concrete problems that cause some potential set of customers significant pain—problems with solutions for which customers would be willing to pay. Serial Innovators know they have an interesting problem when it meets three criteria:

1. Solving the problem has the potential for significant financial impact.

2. A solution likely can be found.

3. The problem and its solution are acceptable to both customers and management (it solves their problems and fits strategy).

Serial Innovators follow Thomas Edison's advice regarding innovating: "I don't want to invent something that no one will buy." They understand that technology is just a means to an end, the firm is in business to make money, and the only way they will be allowed to continue innovating is to develop a product that profitably solves customer problems.

Serial Innovators typically have lists of potentially important problems they want to explore in the future. They are not pursuing some of these projects at the moment because, at this point in time, they just technically are not feasible. They are not pursuing other projects because they do not fit with the firm's strategy, or because the timing is not right from an economic perspective:

There is a lot of timing involved, because you can have a brilliant idea, but if the company is struggling to make a profit at that point, they can't take on that new idea. If their plate is already full, and it takes that three years or five years to get something to the pipeline, then it's pretty hard to step ahead.

However, not even successful Serial Innovators can always define their own work. On average, the problem arose from an identified new technology capability about one-third of the time, the Serial Innovator identified the potential problem through their marketplace knowledge one-third of the time, and the final one-third of the time, someone from management assigned them a problem on which to work. However, even when management assigned them a problem to investigate, the Serial Innovator nearly always reframed the problem and took his or her investigation in an unanticipated direction—not because the Innovator selfishly wanted to define the direction of the work, but because he or she had come to understand the customer need more deeply. For example, one senior manager's initial directive to a Serial Innovator to improve laptop lightbulb performance ultimately evolved into a project focused on laptop power management more generally.

Finding the right problem is nontrivial and does not lend itself to an easily duplicated formula. All Serial Innovators told stories of expending significant time and effort toward the pursuit of a solution, only to discover they had been working on the wrong problem from the beginning. Keys to successfully finding good problems include

- Having a depth of knowledge and focus in a particular technical domain;
- Additional technical knowledge from peripheral domains;
- Deep customer knowledge; and
- A tolerance for ambiguity.

This combination of knowledge and characteristics allows Serial Innovators to see problems that others cannot.

Approaches for Uncovering Potentially Interesting Problems
Serial Innovators use multiple approaches to uncover potentially interesting problems, and then evaluate them against the three criteria listed at the bottom of Figure 2.2. We identified five methods used individually and in combination by Serial Innovators searching for the "right" problem:

1. Approach from a strategic technology perspective.
2. Reframe the current problem.
3. Work backward from a far-into-the-future vision.
4. Use other domains as a resource.
5. The problem is given.

In addition, Serial Innovators almost always start from customer problems and look for unarticulated customer needs by asking broad and deep questions.

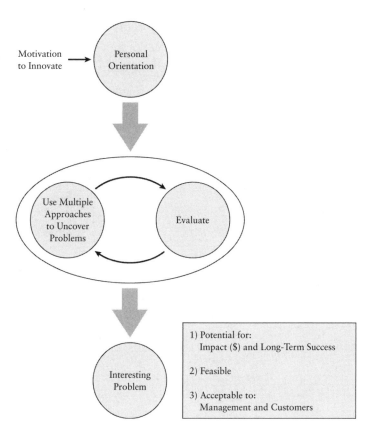

FIGURE 2.2   Find the right problem

Using Strategy to Identify Problems.   Sometimes Serial Innovators, like Inventors, start investigating a problem area because the performance capabilities of a particular technology have reached a plateau, while performance demands keep increasing. To move to the next performance level requires shifting to a different technology. For example, as electronics become more sophisticated, complex, and miniaturized, regulating the voltage from power supplies more precisely and efficiently also becomes more important. Power supply voltages initially were regulated by linear regulators, which are analog in nature and markedly inefficient. To take voltage regulation to a higher level of performance, one Serial Innovator knew he would have to change technologies—analog performance would not work. He ultimately found a way to combine analog and digital components to solve the problem.

Reframe Existing Problems.   Serial Innovators have an uncanny ability to reframe existing problems. By immersing themselves in a problem, they see it through a different lens that allows them to capture aspects that had been previously overlooked. For example, Tom Osborn, a chemist by training, transformed what seemed to be a chemical problem in feminine care—what material(s) can we use to capture this fluid more effectively?—into one of human factors and physiology—how does the fluid actually flow from the body and onto the feminine hygiene pad? Once he reframed the parameters of the problem, he was able to imagine solutions that had never before been considered.

Work Backward from a Far-in-the-Future Vision.   Serial Innovators may work backward from a long-term goal to discover how tackling a series of short-term problems might allow them to ultimately produce, many decades later, that long-term vision. They would begin by developing a salable product based on the first technology step, providing a pathway of interesting (i.e., profit-producing) shorter-term problems to solve on the way toward their long-term end point.

Our favorite story of this approach is about Adam Gudat, a Serial Innovator at Caterpillar, whose vision was to be able to drop a set of machines into a completely remote area and then fly into the airport they had created, with no human intervention, two years later. Working backward, he determined that he would first need to know where equipment was located geographically. From there, Adam would have to remotely drive and control equipment according to precise geographic coordinates.

So Adam began creating GPS-based navigation systems for heavy equipment, starting with farm equipment. Follow-on projects combining those GPS navigation systems with satellite mapping capabilities, various soil and moisture sensors, and other technologies ultimately has created "precision farming," which is revolutionizing agribusiness, especially in the Midwest. The technologies now can allow farmers to map the conditions of their fields specifically, and then vary the rate of fertilization according to the need identified by GPS-guided grid or zone sampling. Fertilizer is spread only in areas that need it, optimizing its use and increasing farmer profitability while providing entirely new revenue and profit streams for Caterpillar. No, the company does not yet have the ability to create a whole airport remotely, but they are clearly advancing toward that vision and reshaping the agriculture industry on the way.

Use Other Domains for Insight.   Serial Innovators find the right problem by gathering insight from across multiple domains. Fred, a Serial Innovator in medical devices, routinely tracked university patent applications in his search for interesting problems. He initiated conversations with university Inventors to determine what they were doing and, more important, *why*. The "why" gave him insight into what problems these university Inventors thought were important. He also routinely visited university new venture incubators, investigating why they were trying to commercialize the various technologies—what problems were they trying to solve? When he found multiple academic researchers patenting and trying to commercialize different products to solve similar problems, he knew he was on track to finding an interesting problem to solve for the firm.

Management Dictates the Problem.   Finally, problems also are given to the Serial Innovator by management. The problem could be passed on from another unit within the organization or could arise from a new industry or government standard that requires a breakthrough new solution, such as more exacting emissions regulations for engines. In some of these cases, the "interesting" problem is created externally to the organization. Alternatively, the problem may be suggested by a manager, based on their experience.

Jim, an electronics industry Serial Innovator, had no idea that liquid crystal displays (LCDs) even had lightbulbs in them when his manager one day asked him, "Have you ever thought about lighting off lightbulbs in liquid crystal displays?" After his manager suggested that "you should think about it because there are a lot of liquid crystal displays around and there are going to be a lot more," Jim starting looking into how to illuminate LCDs. And he found that, indeed, illuminating them was an issue.

Even when given a problem, Serial Innovators still spend significant time confirming that it is indeed interesting. For example, Jim took nearly nine months investigating the problem of illuminating LCDs before he came to his conclusions:

- Yes, the market for LCDs was sizable and growing rapidly.
- The current illumination solution was inefficient, costly, and limited battery longevity in laptops.
- No one else was paying attention to it.
- It looked like a significantly improved solution was feasible.

In other words, it took him nine months to confirm that the problem was "interesting," based on the three criteria presented in Figure 2.2. Managers need to understand that Serial Innovators will find a way to *not* work on a problem that they have been given if their preliminary investigation determines the problem to be uninteresting.

Regardless of the approaches used to find the right problem, Serial Innovators continuously evaluate the problems they find before moving forward. Evaluation happens in parallel. Once they think they have identified a possible problem of interest, Serial Innovators solicit feedback from a variety of sources to help them evaluate its true worth. They may consult people with marketing, manufacturing, and technical backgrounds, as well as those with financial backgrounds to help them understand the financial implications of the project. Additionally, they will repeatedly question potential customers about the importance of the problem they are considering tackling.

Be Flexible in Using and Combining Problem-Finding Approaches

Some of the problem-finding approaches may be more appropriate than others for a given situation, and no one approach is guaranteed to help identify interesting problems every time a Serial Innovator goes looking for one. Thus, Serial Innovators are flexible in how they apply these approaches, frequently combining several in their search, or moving from one to another when the first approach does not result in an interesting problem.

Serial Innovators continue to use multiple approaches until they find a problem that promises to be interesting for the firm. Only when a problem meeting all three criteria is identified will the Serial Innovators shift their actions from the objective of "finding" to "understanding."

UNDERSTAND THE PROBLEM DEEPLY

To deeply understand something you have to live it.

As with finding an interesting problem, Serial Innovators use a series of approaches for understanding the problem completely. They first prepare to understand the problem by defining what they need to know and assembling the team of people who will help them achieve this knowledge, as shown in the oval to the left in Figure 2.3. They use these assets to think holistically about the problem. They also choose from several techniques to integrate knowledge from four domains: customers' perspectives, technical perspectives, market opportunities, and competitors' positions, as illustrated on the right side of Figure 2.3. Although their focus primarily iterates between understanding the customer and the technical perspectives of the problem, as we indicate in Figure 1.6, Serial Innovators do make occasional forays into understanding the market in aggregate and competitive positions to ensure that the problem remains interesting and unsolved. They oscillate between increasing their understanding of the problem from these multiple domains and adapting the resources they need to obtain that knowledge, as illustrated in Figure 2.3. At some point, they conclude that they have reduced the unknowns sufficiently to proceed toward inventing a solution to the problem: they have created a path toward innovation, as depicted at the bottom of Figure 2.3.

Prepare to Understand

In preparing to understand, Serial Innovators do not rely solely on themselves to define the problem and its unknowns. Part of their preparation includes assembling the people they need from the various domains that will help them completely understand the problem. Most frequently, they create a "team" of people in their network not formally assigned to the project, who they tap—sometimes individually, sometimes in groups—to help clarify various aspects of the problem. Then, with the help of their "team," Serial Innovators define what they need to know. Some Serial Innovators use the technique of asking the "why" question five times, "peeling the onion" to understand root causes. Another Serial Innovator puts together a "learning plan," a simple document or presentation in which he and his team agree to and write down what they know as well as what they do not

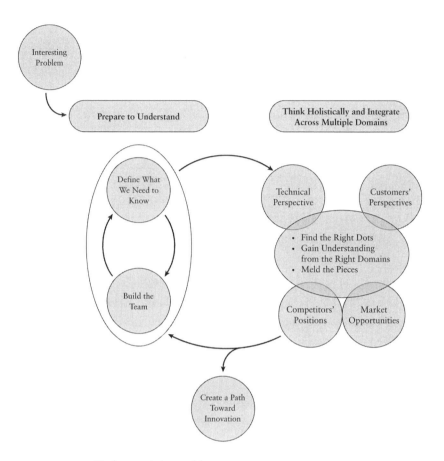

FIGURE 2.3   Understand the problem

know about the problem, the project, and its objectives. Serial Innovators believe there is more power in understanding what they do not know than what they already do, so they tend to focus on the "what don't we know."

Once they have defined the initial unknowns and assembled the resources necessary to eliminate them, they start the work of gathering and synthesizing information to eliminate the unknowns.

Think Holistically Across Multiple Domains
Serial Innovators gather information from a number of perspectives and then integrate across those multiple domains to understand completely, as illustrated in the right side of Figure 2.3. They speak of thinking holisti-

cally to "connect the dots," the specific pieces of information associated with understanding the problem. But, in order to connect them, they first must "find the dots." The task at hand is all about discovery. In their form of discovering, the real challenge is to view the problem from multiple perspectives, or domains. They think from the technical, customer, market, and competitive perspectives, melding information from each into an overall, holistic understanding of the problem and the various contexts in which it resides. Problems are viewed as more than technical or engineering challenges; they are multifaceted systems.

Unlike typical technology push breakthrough innovation projects, in which discovery involves just the ability to "seek out and develop foundational knowledge in the basic disciplines associated with the domain, recognize opportunities, and articulate opportunities" (O'Connor et al. 2008, 53–54), discovery for Serial Innovators means creating an in-depth understanding across four kinds of knowledge, only one of which is technical in nature.

Of course, even in the process of breakthrough innovation, all of the relevant technical "dots" must be understood. Serial Innovators are technical experts in their fields. They have spent many years learning science and engineering; however, they acquire the appropriate technical understanding needed for each problem in different ways than other technologists. First, they tend to go back to the fundamental principles behind complex technical concepts. When an agribusiness firm was looking to develop a new cooking oil that would minimize what was stored in the body as fat, Mark, the Serial Innovator on the project, found a possible candidate in the diacylglycerol chemical family. However, very little was known about this class of oils and their chemistry in the United States, as all the research on them had been done in Japan. To ensure that he understood the fundamentals, Mark volunteered to edit an English-language scientific book about these oils from a clinical and safety standpoint and from a product application standpoint. The endeavor provided him with the fundamental knowledge that allowed him to recommend that the firm move forward with the product.

Additionally, modeling information is a key tool in understanding the fundamental principles of any given problem. Serial Innovators use models to effectively characterize the data from several overlapping perspectives, creating a richer understanding of the problem as a whole. When no model exists, they create one. Their interpretation of what the data reveal allows them to achieve a greater level of understanding. For example, Dave was asked to improve significantly the consistency of nut quality in a nut roasting process. Nut roasting had been thought to be an "art," with many uncontrollable factors changing the roasting rate. This preconception frequently resulted in batches of nuts that had to be thrown away because they were burned or reroasted because they were underdone. In trying to understand the nut roasting process, Dave ran a set of twenty-seven experiments that systematically altered six process variables, including uncontrollable environmental variables such as ambient humidity and temperature. Ultimately, he produced an elegant equation of the relationships among all of the variables—a total understanding of the system. The results of his model allowed the company to nearly eliminate nut defects while simultaneously increasing the absolute capacity of the roasting equipment fourfold.

Unlike pure technologists (Inventors), Serial Innovators seek technical understanding but also recognize the importance of customer and end-consumer derived information in developing their understanding of a problem. At this point, the Serial Innovator is not trying to market a product—just trying to understand the problem from the customer's perspective. Serial Innovators perform their own market research instead of letting a separate division or outside firm conduct research for them. They need richness in the data, and they need to understand it personally. They cannot let other people interpret raw data for them.

Tom Osborn, whose story we told in the Introduction, described his passion for understanding his customer as stemming from the desire to have every product be a "cherished gift" for her. He wanted every interaction to be the equivalent of "sending her a love letter." While these statements are striking, even provocative, we think the words he uses and the way he expresses his need to understand his customers differentiate the Serial Innovator's approach from the conventional marketing theory of having a customer or marketing orientation. Serial Innovators go far beyond having a market orientation; they practice "customer immersion." The customer immersion practices in which they engage are so numerous and important that Chapter 3 is devoted solely to explicating them.

In addition to technical and customer perspectives, Serial Innovators have a keen awareness of their competitor's capabilities. Jim, in developing an understanding of the illumination of LCDs in laptop screens, bought and tore apart every brand of laptop available on the market to understand the decisions competitors had made. He found that all of their solutions were inefficient and simplistic, further leading him to believe that this function could be important to innovate. Other Serial Innovators kept notebooks for each of their competitors with the last five to six years of new product designs, specifications, and feature trade-offs detailed through reverse engineering. Serial Innovators understand how technology—both theirs and their competitors'—fits into the market. They understand the trade-offs between the two, and are able to find the right balance between their technology and the demands of the market. They then use the insight they acquire by intensely studying their customers to give them an advantage over the products their competitors have engineered.

During this "dot-finding" process, Serial Innovators focus primarily on understanding individual customer needs and technical possibilities and on maintaining a sense of what competitors are doing. However, they occasionally circle back into considering the general market trends to ensure that there still is a market for the problem they are trying to solve—and that someone else has not already commercialized a product to solve that problem, as is illustrated in Figure 1.6. During this part of the process, Serial Innovators look at individual customers to understand specific needs. To understand market opportunities, on the other hand, they look at the market in aggregate.

The key to complete problem understanding involves more than gathering information from all four domains. As with the relationships among the overall innovation tasks illustrated in Figure 2.1, understanding the problem is an inherently circular process. As Serial Innovators refine their understanding of the problem from each perspective, they redefine their objectives and enhance their support network. Then, when they have gathered sufficient information across all relevant dimensions, Serial Innovators make connections across these disparate types of information that others just do not see. Their special capability to synthesize information allows them to reach the desired "Aha!" moment needed to solve the problem. We've labeled this capability "discernment," as it involves keen insight on the part of the Serial Innovator in order to see the solution of a profoundly complex problem with a multitude of constraints.

When we have asked Serial Innovators about this capability, they typically shrug their shoulders; "I've been told it's a gift," is one reply. They don't know how they do it either. We tentatively conclude that they have gathered enough breadth and depth of knowledge through their multifaceted investigation of each problem that they can make an experience-based intuitive leap. This leap is possible in part because of their capabilities, and in part because management has granted them enough time and sufficient resources to truly understand the problem at hand.

Creating a Path Toward Innovation

One Serial Innovator described his goal for understanding as needing to make the problem simple enough that it can be explained to his boss, to his boss's boss, and to his spouse. As in the "opportunity articulation" of discovery in O'Conner et al. (2008), Serial Innovators know that they understand all of the tricky, specific details of a problem when they can get intelligent but less technical others to understand what the problem is and why it is compelling. Yet whereas a technology push project has a specific technical solution and not much market information at the opportunity articulation stage, Serial Innovators have a significant amount of market and customer information but no technical solution to the problem at this stage. The Serial Innovator has now developed enough information, however, to create a path toward innovation that allows him or her to shift to the tasks of inventing to solve that problem.

INVENT AND VALIDATE

After spending significant time and resources selecting and understanding the right problem, Serial Innovators move on to inventing solutions to that problem, as illustrated in Figure 2.4. The challenge of the invent-and-validate portion of the process involves translating the understanding of the problem (created in the previous phases) into a concrete proposed

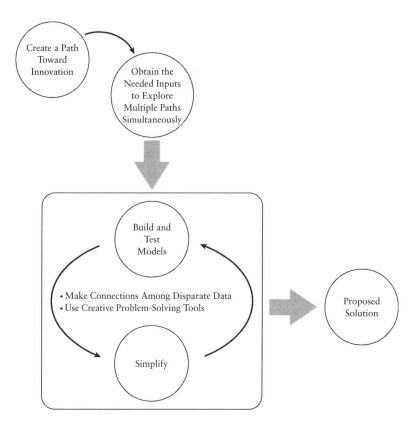

FIGURE 2.4   Invent and validate

solution that can be acted upon by the rest of the company. This effort usually begins by taking the identified paths toward innovation; pursuing those paths to determine what is feasible; building qualitative models of the problem and proposed solutions; and then enhancing those models quantitatively to work toward a simple, elegant answer that provides a holistic solution to the problem. Ultimately, Serial Innovators produce a proposed solution in the form of a new product or service, which is then shifted into the firm's formal NPD process for execution, physical development, and commercialization. Needless to say, this phase brings everything into focus and determines if the understanding and the initial ideas will be valuable for the firm.

Explore Multiple Paths Simultaneously

Serial Innovators recognize that there may be several potential solutions to their problem. To avoid anchoring on initially proposed solutions without fully understanding other approaches, Serial Innovators frequently set up multiple parallel approaches to invention, using different scientific trajectories. For example, Ted, a Serial Innovator at a consumer packaged goods company, found from working with housewives that plastic wrap did not really work effectively. Either it sticks to nothing and slides off of the bowls people are trying to cover or it sticks to everything—but mostly to itself. His goal was thus to develop a product that did not tangle when coming off of the roll, but that created a good seal when pressed lightly against a surface. Completely unsure of what approach to take, he assembled one team consisting primarily of mechanical engineers with whom he investigated possible mechanical solutions to the problem, one team of predominantly chemists and material scientists with whom he investigated polymeric solutions to the problem, and a final team of chemists and mechanical engineers with whom he investigated a hybrid approach to solving the problem by using some mechanical process changes in combination with a chemical coating. It was ultimately this final team that created the best-performing and most manufacturable solution, which was in fact commercialized and has led to a sizable revenue stream over the years.

The philosophy behind this approach is not to set efforts up in a win–lose competition, but to determine if different scientific approaches could provide a solution to the problem. If both solutions "work," then the cheapest or best of the two can be moved forward to development, with the second solution waiting in the wings in case obstructions to the first are later uncovered. This multipronged development approach actually reflects the findings of previous research: research and development (R&D) teams that pursued two potential approaches simultaneously produced more successful solutions than those pursuing only one potential solution at a time (Allen 1966).

As Serial Innovators pursue the innovation paths they have identified, they are constantly working on several challenges associated with the path to innovation:

- Defining and understanding constraints that limit the usefulness of an approach;
- Repurposing what is already available; and
- Expanding the innovative arena by drawing inputs from analogous domains.

Defining and Understanding Constraints.   To begin, Serial Innovators must work within two sets of constraints, which they may have to take some time to clarify: the constraints of nature and those of the firm. First, fundamental scientific principles preclude taking some invention pathways. As one Serial Innovator said: "If a solution to this problem involves using antimatter, it's probably not going to be a good solution."

And although, as we will see below, Serial Innovators frequently do expand the firm's technology domains in seeking solutions, they also understand that sometimes the firm's strategy or intrinsic technical capabilities just will not allow them to pursue a particular type of solution; they typically think about constraints as restrictions "for now." Firm policy may force Serial Innovators to shelve further action toward a particular concept, or to change innovation paths. That does not mean, however, that the Serial Innovator may not revisit this technology pathway at some later date, if the firm has expanded its capabilities or evolved its strategy. For Serial Innovators, inventing is as much about ruling out what cannot be done as it is about determining what can be done.

Repurposing What Is Already Available.   Fundamentally, Serial Innovators only invent when they really have to, because invention is hard work, plus it takes time and consumes resources. Serial Innovators display a tendency to repurpose what they already have whenever possible.

Take the example of Mark in the food oils business. Rather than starting off down a chemical synthesis path to create a new moiety to achieve the project goal, he first searched globally for any material already in existence that could potentially solve the problem, even though that product might currently be used for some other application. In other words, Mark looked to customer needs for inspiration (lower-fat cooking oils), but looked outside of the company for a potential solution already available.

The key to his success was that he flexibly repurposed this initial material, tweaking it as necessary to create the product most appropriate for his particular application. By repurposing an existing product, Mark also saved development time and money that might have been spent by starting an invention from scratch.

Move Outside the Firm's Current Technology Arena.   Serial Innovators invent more successfully when they are not bound by the norms of what is currently technologically acceptable in their organizations. Rather, successful Serial Innovators expand their innovative arenas to new technology domains when needed and invent from a systems perspective. Consider the example of stents for keeping blood vessels open after arteriosclerosis plaque has been removed. Medical device firms first used a pure materials solution to this problem—a stent, or metal tube, that holds the artery or vein open. However, over time, stent manufacturers found that a significant number of patients suffered from restenosis, a second narrowing of the blood vessels, sometime after they had received this purely mechanical solution. In order to improve patient care and prevent restenosis, manufacturers moved into a new technical arena (for them), adding pharmaceutical development and clinical testing capabilities to develop drug-eluting stents, which solved the restenosis problem from a different scientific perspective. Stent companies that could not move into the new technology arena found themselves materially disadvantaged in the marketplace.

Drawing from Analogous Domains.   Other Serial Innovators are adept at using analogous domains for finding inputs to the invention process. Looking within their own industries for new ideas frequently is not useful. The same suppliers often are used industry-wide—any new knowledge created by a supplier typically spreads to all in the industry and does not provide a competitive advantage to any one firm. Thus, Serial Innovators look for noncompeting industries with a similar problem and investigate those industries' alternative solutions to that problem.

For example, consider the diaper industry, which uses high-speed papermaking equipment. A Serial Innovator whose current process is limiting him or her from producing a breakthrough new diaper concept may look to the high-end magazine publishing industry or to the photographic film industry because these fields use similar production processes. Similarly, when Adam Gudat at Caterpillar envisioned remote-controlled machines building an airport, but found no robotic capabilities in the firm, he turned to the U.S. government laboratories and found a researcher at Oak Ridge National Labs who was "playing around with robots that were pushing a pencil around on the floor." This robot was designed on a much smaller scale than Adam needed, but its task was fully analogous to his own. This researcher's efforts gave Adam the technical start he needed for advancing his vision into developing precision farming equipment.

Build and Test Models

Serial Innovators use models of potential solutions to help them invent for a number of reasons. Models are a tool for quantifying the "unquantifiable." They first create basic models and then use divergent thinking to add variables until they encompass the entire problem system. Serial Innovators typically start with "qualitative modeling" to understand the bigger picture of what is happening in their system. Qualitative modeling creates pictorial representations of aspects of a problem that support reasoning with very little quantitative information. Tom Osborn's qualitative model of menstruation changed when he started to think qualitatively from the "drop of fluid" perspective. How does that somewhat viscous drop travel through the body and get onto the pad? What causes it to slide off the pad and go elsewhere? This model change started the process of quantitatively modeling where and how fluids needed to be captured in a feminine pad. The power of qualitative modeling is potentially enormous.

Serial Innovators use models for many reasons, such as to

- Challenge assumptions;
- Test hypotheses;
- Look at the solution as a system; and
- Reconnect with customers to better understand their needs.

Ultimately, Serial Innovators use models to predict the future, allowing them to fail early and cheaply, before large resource investments are required.

Models Challenge Assumptions.   Dave, our Serial Innovator improving the nut roasting process, modeled it experimentally to test ingoing assumptions (from theory, manufacturing experience, and naïve intuition) about which factors affect nut roasting outcomes. His set of experiments definitively demonstrated which environmental, equipment, and process-related variables materially impacted nut roast quality, and which did not. Building this exhaustive model allowed him to understand how to change the process to achieve step-function changes in nut quality and roasting efficiencies simultaneously.

Models Test Hypotheses.   Inventors and basic scientists frequently run experiments in which they have no idea about what the outcome might be when they are seeking new technology capabilities. Consider the process by which many pharmaceutical firms traditionally have developed new drugs. They start by randomly synthesizing thousands of new molecules at a time, and then test each one against the particular virus or disease they are trying to cure. Serial Innovators work differently, having expectations when they run tests. They create experiments and build models specifically to test hypotheses, which means that they start from fundamental science(s) to create those hypotheses. They then use their findings as another opportunity for generating further understanding.

Models to Investigate the Solution as a System.   Models also support inventing from a systems perspective to get at the breakthrough possibilities, rather than feature by feature. Whereas physical prototypes of various features can be inexpensive to create, a modifiable prototype of a complex product or entire system can be very expensive. For example, in optimizing a manufacturing processing line, physically optimizing one machine on the line is not difficult. However, the single improved machine creates an operational "local optima," which may not produce an operational "global optima."

Serial Innovators use design of experiment methodologies (Kuehl 1999) to model total systems. When the product or process is too complex to model experimentally, they turn to system simulation methodologies to help them develop potential solutions. For example, before attempting a live demonstration of remotely operating heavy equipment, Adam Gudat and his team created a software tool that produced a simulation of that task. Ultimately, the software was capable of

running five [simulated] bulldozers dozing an area, nobody controlling them, all computers controlling, machines talking to each other, telling what they were doing, how they were progressing on the database, on the progress of it. And if one machine got into trouble, couldn't do the job . . . it would broadcast to the rest of the machines.

Using Models to Reconnect with Customers.   Interestingly, not only did Adam's software tool allow his team to move into physical invention for the system, it also allowed them to reconnect with potential customers and to understand their needs more fully. Viewing this simulation, with its task-limited capabilities, allowed customers to help the team prioritize what other remotely controlled tasks would be most beneficial for them.

Simplify

> It starts out fuzzy, usually with a few variables. And then over time it evolves and becomes more and more complex. And then all of a sudden, usually what happens is the weight of the model is just too great. It breaks down. And I have to remake a new model. Simpler.

Models start out simple. A qualitative model is a simple pictorial representation. The first quantitative models that Serial Innovators build also start simply. However, as they move from modeling subsystems of solutions to the entire system, models evolve in complexity. Ultimately, models may become complex and even nonlinear, with circularity and feedback loops that are even more complicated than our hourglass model of Serial Innovator innovation. When models become too large and begin to break down, Serial Innovators start over from a more elementary position, utilizing what they have learned to enhance the new model.

Simplifying requires the reapplication of creative and intuitive insights, using them to make new connections across various domains and technologies to make their models more elegant. None of the Serial Innovators described their problems as "easy," but many of them were able to simplify very complex problems into manageable models.

Methods for Inventing and Validating

Serial Innovators iterate between building and testing models of solutions to the problem and continuing to try and simplify that solution so that it is acceptable to customers and to the management of the firm. Two of the many methods they use include making connections among disparate data and creative problem-solving techniques.

Making Connections Among Disparate Data.   The process of invention can be viewed as making a series of connections between previously dissimilar concepts and technologies to assemble all or parts of them into a never-before-seen solution. This ability to connect disparate pieces of information in new ways—"discernment"—is a characteristic that differentiates Serial Innovators from other technologists (see Chapter 5 for a fuller explanation and Chapter 6 for more on how to determine who has this characteristic and who does not). Synthesizing information from many different sources, Serial Innovators continuously make connections as they invent and validate. Several of them articulated their connection-making process by using very colorful metaphors.

Sandra, another consumer packaged goods Serial Innovator, talked about having "fuzzy dust balls" hanging in 3-D space that she continuously was learning more about, to make them a bit more solid than fuzzy. As they hung there, she also moved them around visually in her mind, looking for connections between them. Her connection process is a bit like playing 3-D chess—looking for moves not just left, right, or laterally, but also up and down. Her connection-making "model" has an almost organic quality, allowing for the possibility of spontaneous synthesis, but at the same time requiring a significant effort to "solidify the fuzzy dust balls."

Another Serial Innovator used a fishing metaphor about making connections. He talked about having "a bunch of bobbers hanging in the water that have little thoughts attached to them. And when you make the connection, you pull one of those things up and then a bunch of stuff is hanging on it. And then you look through that stuff to see how it connects to another bobber."

Whether using "fuzzy dust balls" or "floating bobbers," all Serial Innovators focused considerable time and energy understanding and modeling the relationships between the pieces of their problem. Seeing these connections is the catalyst for their inventive actions.

Use Creative Problem-Solving Techniques.   Creative problem solving uses various techniques to generate a divergent set of potential problem solutions, and then to converge on the solution that best meets the firm's capabilities, customer needs, and the current state of technology (De Bono 1973; Treffinger et al. 2006). Creative problem-solving techniques also allow Serial Innovators to invent from a systems perspective. That is, rather than inventing feature by feature, they believe that the power to get to breakthrough invention lies in inventing at the overall functional level.

Tom Osborn articulated that breakthrough invention results from more than just considering solutions for feature A, then feature B, and then feature C. He finds that the key insights to being able to create breakthrough inventions come from looking at what he called the "cross terms" between the different parts of the problem: A * B; B * C; and A * C. These "cross terms" were not necessarily specific variables in an overall equation; they constituted seemingly unrelated pieces of the problem, at least from a scientific perspective. He finds that achieving breakthrough innovation requires divergent thinking to invent at the interfaces where scientific domains overlap from a needs perspective. For example, when working on feminine hygiene pads, the overlapping fields were garment design, material absorbency, and the physiology of fluid release. Although the previous research in this product area had focused only on more effective fluid capture, Tom identified the potential in these other scientific domains after reframing the problem to one of understanding fluid flow and how clothes and the body interact. This ability to work creatively across divergent scientific fields led to his breakthroughs. Creating breakthrough innovations at the systems level requires inputs from multiple scientific domains that are creatively combined.

The Fuzzy Front End Outcome: A Proposed Solution to the Problem
Ultimately, after considerable iteration and efforts in understanding, inventing, and validating, the Serial Innovator proposes a solution to the interesting problem. The FFE of innovation has become less fuzzy. The

proposed solution is ready to move into the implementation phase of product development, which, in the best-case scenario, will turn the solution into a manufacturable and salable product.

To move into physical development, the project first must be accepted into the firm's new product pipeline. Senior management must be sold on its potential value to the firm, feasibility, and fit with strategy. This task is inherently a political one, which successful Serial Innovators have been actively engaging throughout the FFE. Chapter 4 details the different types of activities that Serial Innovators use to gain political acceptance for their projects.

EXECUTE: PHYSICALLY DEVELOP THE PRODUCT

The firm's standardized and formal NPD methods now are appropriate for managing the rest of development, as many more organizational resources—including people from many different functions, engineering design systems, and manufacturing facilities for pilot production—are needed to further develop the proposed solution into a commercially viable product. However, the Serial Innovators do not "hand off" the project once they have "solved" the problem. On the contrary, they take an active role both in project execution and then in creating acceptance in the market, as shown in Figure 2.1.

This sustained commitment to a project distinguishes how Serial Innovators innovate, compared to the more typical pathway a technology push innovation takes as described by both Markham (2002) and O'Connor et al. (2008). The Serial Innovator's personal involvement in product execution eliminates the need to find someone to champion the transition across the Valley of Death (Markham 2002) or from incubation to acceleration* (O'Connor et al. 2008).

Figure 2.5 illustrates the Serial Innovators' view of project execution. While the internal part of the funnel looks very much like three of the stages in the standard linear Stage-Gate process of Figure 1.1, Serial Innovators see four additional tasks that also must be undertaken.

---

* In the O'Connor et al. (2008) view of technology-driven radical innovation, incubation is the stage where the breakthrough innovation evolves into a bona fide business proposition. Acceleration ramps up the business opportunity to stand on its own.

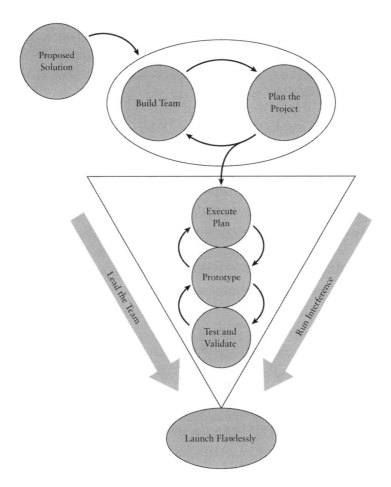

FIGURE 2.5 Execute

The first pair of tasks before physical implementation starts is building the team and planning the project. Whereas most firms' NPD processes include these tasks implicitly, they are explicitly and separately addressed in Serial Innovators' processes. And although it is not clear in most firms "who" is responsible for assigning and assembling the team and creating the project plan, Serial Innovators firmly believe that it is their personal responsibility.

Serial Innovators find that "volunteers" exert more and better effort than managerially assigned personnel. They work very hard, using their informal networks and the goodwill they have generated over time by helping others throughout the firm solve various technical problems, to recruit volunteers for their project. Adam Gudat of Caterpillar describes how he gathers volunteers:

I did and do a lot of face-to-face. I hate telephones. I hate e-mail. The only way I have worked is always go over there . . . Muhammad goes to the mountain and I go to wherever I need to go to sit down and talk to them 'cause I want to see their reaction when I propose something, and if I see it's misunderstood, I can at least explain something or we can try another angle of it.

They also take extraordinary steps to meld the set of individuals into a team. For example, Frank, a Serial Innovator in a heavy equipment company, had each of the individuals in one of his projects create a quilt block that depicted how they believed their function would contribute to the overall project. None of his all-male engineering/design/manufacturing team had ever made a quilt before. As you can imagine, the team was skeptical about the value of the endeavor. Frank was not a quilter, but as a quilter's husband he had seen the community-building that such a joint endeavor can produce. When the team members completed their blocks, Frank's wife assembled them into the quilt and sewed it. The quilt, which hung in their team room for the duration of the project, ended up being a rallying point and a vehicle that helped the whole team articulate and integrate across the various facets of the project.

Serial Innovators also take responsibility for developing the plan for execution. They are not control freaks—indeed, they typically are happy turning the day-to-day facilitation of the execution phase over to a professional project manager—but at this point in the project, they know more than anyone else about what needs to be done and what types of functions and resources are likely to be needed. Of course, they are not masters of all functional areas, and thus, to detail various parts of the plan, they enlist the help of their more functionally knowledgeable team members. They turn to their manufacturing teammates for details on the tasks and timing for manufacturing development, pilot, and scale-up, and to their marketing teammates for information on marketing tasks and timing. But the Serial Innovator takes the responsibility for ensuring that the product plan does not overlook any critical factors.

Even though the project's day-to-day tasks are most likely to be run by a professional project manager, Serial Innovators provide leadership to the team and keep lines of communication open with senior management to ensure that the necessary resources continue to be available to execute the plan. Their team leader role differs from the project management role, which ensures that all of the details of the project plan get executed. The team leader is less of an executive and more of a leader and ambassador role. Adam Gudat's description of this role is compelling:

You've got to be right there with them through thick and thin, through good news and bad news, and there are times when they're frustrated and so you have to be there . . . to listen to them. You have to learn with them. You have to encourage them. You have to feed them in the middle of the night, lots of pizza and beer, root beer runs.

He found that showing the team his undying passion for the project throughout execution was crucial to keeping the team engaged through the tedious aspects of development and through various technical and material obstacles. He also procured emergency access to special equipment or manufacturing pilot time as required, relying on his network and contacts to get special access.

Throughout the entire execution process, while leading the team, Serial Innovators work with customers to create market acceptance, as shown in the bottom circular depiction of Figure 2.1.

CREATING MARKET ACCEPTANCE
In general, NPD teams launch a product, perhaps hold a team closure dinner and postlaunch audit of the process used, and then immediately take up new projects. Their responsibility stops at launch. Serial Innovators, however, follow their products into the marketplace. While they create market acceptance for their product, they also pick up additional information on the problems that still are unsolved for customers, locating other potential opportunities. In fulfilling this objective, they work directly with

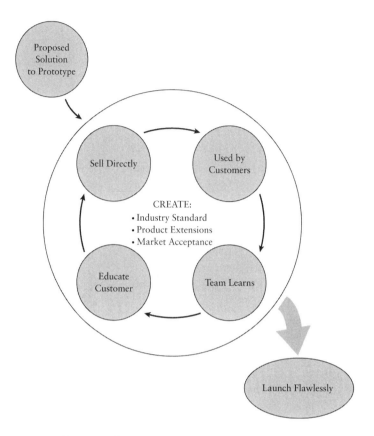

FIGURE 2.6   Create market acceptance

potential customers, educating them on the product and even selling directly to them, as depicted in Figure 2.6. The Serial Innovator shares lessons he or she learns through customer interaction with the entire team, because the team members will be responsible for the next set of product iterations and for improving the product that has been launched.

Customer education appears in many forms, many of which (such as demonstrating and beta testing prototypes) are standard at many firms, whereas others are less conventional. Chuck House, for example, created undergraduate college classes in how to design with some of the various innovative electronic devices he developed. Mark, in agribusiness, ran seminars at customers' development sites that helped them understand emulsifier technology in relationship to other food-thickening mechanisms.

Other Serial Innovators actually traveled with their sales force before launch, educating both the sales force and the customers simultaneously about the new product.

In summary, then, to Serial Innovators, the marketplace problem is not solved until the product is in the hands of the consumer and is achieving expected sales. As shown at the bottom of Figure 2.1, they work iteratively across leading the execution team and simultaneously creating customer acceptance until they are certain that the product is ready to "launch flawlessly." And then, after they have seen the product growing in the market and the development needs have evolved into product extension and incremental improvement tasks, they turn to another problem that is floating in their clouds, bobbing on their bobbers, or sitting on their bookshelves, and they work to innovate again.

SUMMARY

Incremental NPD projects do not have much fuzziness in the front end of the innovation process. The next evolutionary change is usually rather obvious: make the product faster, smaller, or lighter—or continue moving along some other performance trajectory already established in the competitive arena. However, for breakthrough innovations, the front end can be extraordinarily fuzzy. The processes that Serial Innovators use thus differ materially from processes we have seen referred to in the literature on innovation: it is structured and systematic while still being nonlinear and iterative. They focus efforts on the following aspects of development:

- The FFE: finding and understanding interesting problems;
- Inventing and validating solutions for these problems;
- Engaging with customers throughout the process;
- Building, leading, and supporting the execution team; and
- Generating customer and market acceptance.

Serial Innovators expend a significant amount of time finding the "right" problem, which they define as one that has the potential for large impact for the firm, is feasible, and is acceptable to both customers and management. Serial Innovators also spend a significant amount of time ensuring that they understand the problem completely. They circle across these two objectives, refining the problem statement and their understanding of it, until they have created a path toward innovation that lets them move into the tasks of inventing to solve the problem. To the organization, this time can appear as nonmovement. There may be few, if any, visible traces that a new product is being developed.

One key to success at this point in the process is for management to encourage and allow Serial Innovators the time and energy it takes to support this level of understanding. Extreme managerial insight, understanding, and patience are required, as we expand upon in Chapter 7.

A second key to success at this point is ensuring that the Serial Innovator has access to customers, market trend information, and information about the firm's strategy, as we emphasize in Chapter 3. Serial Innovators need to know as much about the business and customer needs as they know about technology.

Inventing and validating a solution to a given problem requires that Serial Innovators use all of the tools of creative problem solving to build and test models of proposed solutions, and that they work to simplify their models of the problem and the solutions they have created. At this point, they need access to potential technology solutions that reside inside—and especially outside—of the organization. Serial Innovators also need to communicate with various individuals with technical expertise outside of their own domain. Finally, they are likely to need experimental equipment and engineering software design and analysis programs that will allow them to model the problems and their potential solutions.

In execution, Serial Innovators focus on obtaining their volunteer team members and melding them into the team, and then on planning the project. Then, they provide project leadership and create market acceptance. At this point in the project, Serial Innovators should not be distracted with new assignments, and they should be allowed to spend additional time in the field, focusing on customer interaction.

The processes these Serial Innovators use start well before the standard formal product development processes used by firms for incremental innovation, and they extend past the typically conceptualized end of product development—the launch. Rather than being linear in nature, they are fully circular and include feedback loops that need to be explicitly acknowledged in their depiction. These Serial Innovators integrate the FFE to the more formal product development process in place in the firm, lead the project during execution, and push the product into the market.

Let us be clear. We are not denigrating or disparaging either the technology push or market pull approach to breakthrough innovation. We view Serial Innovators as a complementary mechanism for creating breakthrough innovations. One or more Serial Innovators likely already reside in every organization. Other aspiring Serial Innovators likely do, too. Our goal in this chapter was to help manage them more effectively by understanding how they develop breakthrough products.

3   CUSTOMER ENGAGEMENT FOR BREAKTHROUGH INNOVATION

Customers* are central to almost everything Serial Innovators do. Serial Innovators are intrinsically driven into solve customer problems. To appreciate fully how important customers are to the innovation process, this chapter describes how Serial Innovators interact with, engage with, learn from, and influence customers. We first describe some assumptions about how engineers deal with customers and why they typically do not interact with customers more often. Then we describe the interactions with customers that Serial Innovators told us are critical for breakthrough innovation. Finally, we provide advice about how Serial Innovators can engage effectively with customers at every step of their innovation process and offer suggestions for managers to facilitate these endeavors.

As discussed in Chapter 2, the process used by Serial Innovators stresses spending significant time up front, prior to physically developing a product (see Figure 2.1):

---

* By "customers," we refer to more than just those who currently purchase the firm's products and services. Those individuals are already at least somewhat satisfied by our current product line. "Customers" in this chapter includes anyone or any firm with a set of problems we would like to try and solve. They may be customers of a competitor, or they may not be anyone's customer at this point in time, as there currently is no product on the market that can solve their problem satisfactorily at a price they are willing to pay. We also include internal "customers," such as is the case for innovating manufacturing processes.

- They search broadly to find "important" problems.
- They spend time understanding the problems deeply before inventing a solution.

Once physical development commences, Serial Innovators utilize the firm's formal processes for efficiency. Finally, they work to create market acceptance of the product. Even though the longest time may be spent in the Fuzzy Front End (FFE), customers are integral to each step in this process.

Many companies look to their biggest customers for new ideas, or create customer advisory boards of their "most important" customers to provide input into development. This input usually produces the "first order effects" of a problem—information about incremental improvements or indications of a more important problem. First order effects represent the tip of the iceberg, the obvious information. Most typically, this information drives cost, quality, and evolutionary performance improvements, which are valid and important, but not particularly interesting for breakthrough innovation. Serial Innovators repeatedly stated that you "never ask customers what they want," because they almost always ask for "faster, lighter, cheaper, etc." And specific product ideas that customers do provide typically require substantial development to make them appropriate for broader markets. Current customers are a great resource for engineers to learn the skills required for effective customer interactions and for understanding the improvements necessary for today's products.

Unfortunately, routine feedback from current customers is unlikely to drive breakthrough innovation. There are a mass of interesting and important issues that form the rest of the iceberg, or the "real" cause and effect of what the problem is and why it is that problem that needs to be understood. The challenge to Serial Innovators is to discover the rest of the iceberg and understand how it is formed. However, acquiring those details is even more difficult because, many times, customers cannot clearly explain what they are really trying to achieve. Sometimes they cannot articulate their ideas well; often, they simply do not know what they need. As one Serial Innovator said, "They are wandering in the desert, trying to figure it out," just as he was. In either scenario, customer interactions offer great opportunities for Serial Innovators who are seeking potential breakthrough problems.

How does one get past the "typical" feedback from customers about the current products? Serial Innovators take a distinct approach to get past superficial feedback from customers. They start by seeking "customers of difference," who are not the largest, or the most expert, but who experience significant problems or have issues with a current product. Frequently, the people Serial Innovators talk to in the marketplace are not even customers. They are individuals or organizations who experience the problems that the Serial Innovator is trying to understand, but who are not satisfied with any existing product.

FINDING AND UNDERSTANDING
INDIVIDUAL CUSTOMER PROBLEMS

Each new arena contains a tremendous amount of knowledge about customer needs that Innovators will have to learn. Some technologists allow others to collect data for them. Serial Innovators do not. They personally find out exactly what resonates with the customer:

[B]y making it [the customer interaction] very real and very personal, it forced me to focus on making sure that at the end of the day I didn't need an arbitrary list, that I really knew was meaningless, that was put together by people who thought they knew what they were doing. I was able to boil it down to, "Okay, this is really what we're gonna have to do," and I think that really helped motivate me to keep charging ahead even when things were getting pretty dim.

Serial Innovators also were very clear that marketing, as a function, cannot provide the insights they gained through their own in-depth, rigorous work with customers. For example:

I remember calling up the marketing guy one day and I asked him, I said, "What's the gear factor ratio on this huge fleet out there?" "Oh, they use the sum ratio." "Which numbers?" And he had about five of them there. And I said, "Which is the one they use most?" And my whole strategy was, "What can I do to make that big customer want our product more than the other guy's" because he was buying the other guy's product. And they were just like, "Well," and I was like,

"No, no, I want to know exactly what he buys." I finally had to send an engineer out . . . [Marketing] just assumed these people were telling the right thing. No, no, you have to understand, you have to focus on the detail.

Serial Innovators push beyond the inputs typically provided by marketing because of their curiosity and desire to understand profoundly so that they can make the connections that less detailed data would not produce (Chapter 5). Their curiosity drives them to seek information from many different sources, and their ability to make connections enables them to see patterns and opportunities that other miss. However, this approach to problem definition is time-consuming. It can take six to nine months or more for a Serial Innovator to define and understand a problem, as it took Jim to understand the problem with lighting liquid crystal display (LCD) screens in laptops.

As we indicated in Chapter 2, Serial Innovators engage in customer immersion to understand customer needs in great detail. Customer immersion differs from market or customer orientation (Narver and Slater 1990). Firms with a market orientation generally strive to understand their customers sufficiently to create sustainable superior value for them over the long term. Serial Innovators practicing customer immersion, on the other hand, focus deeply on understanding a particular problem that currently is very important to some specific subset of customers. Their goal is to provide a superior solution to that one problem.

The first step in becoming customer immersed is finding the consumers or firms with the problem. For many Serial Innovators working in consumer goods, such as Tom Osborn working on the problems of menstruating women, consumers with the target problems are all around them and easy to find. Serial Innovators typically start with questions to their family and friends, or take advantage of individuals identified through their firm's standard market research practices and consumer panels. They then use those people to reach out to additional individuals with slightly different or more critical needs.

For Serial Innovators developing breakthrough innovations for firms, however, the identification process is more complex. First, the appropriate firms must be identified, and then the right people to talk to in the firms must be found. For Jim, looking at powering LCD screens, the firms were laptop producers—easy to identify from the business press. However, he then had to figure out who to talk to in each firm. Was it the primary project manager for the next-generation design? Or the electrical engineer charged with designing the power source? Or was it someone else entirely?

Sometimes the firm's sales force can help locate the right individual to talk to. However, salespeople may not want the Serial Innovator speaking with just any customer, and thus are likely to direct him or her only to their "best" customers. These contacts are likely already satisfied with the products the firm produces and may not prove to be useful. Unfortunately, obtaining customer contacts from the sales force is typically not as useful as digging them up by other means; Serial Innovators' personal networks, both those inside and outside their home firms, are most important in helping them efficiently locate the right individuals in the right companies. However, even with those contacts helping out, finding the right individuals requires a significant amount of phone calling, "snowballing" from one contact to another until they find the most useful people to talk to about the problem. Patience and perseverance are required.

Customer immersion also involves getting to know the customers or potential customers who have been identified as useful contacts: (1) Who, as an individual, are you talking to? (2) What are they interested in? (3) What are their capabilities? and (4) What are they passionate about? These questions *build rapport*, creating an emotional basis between the customer and Serial Innovator. Customers have to believe the Innovator really wants to know them, and that he or she will do something useful with the information they provide. Serial Innovators see their jobs as realizing customer dreams through product development. This task demands exploration, trust building, and mutual understanding.

Most often, once contacts have been identified, the Serial Innovator begins by observing them and asking lots of "why" questions. *Observation* is critical to exploring phenomena, the first dimension of building rapport. By watching and probing a situation or an interaction, the Serial Innovator comes to fully comprehend it. In the beginning, it is not much talking—just watching and then probing.

For example, Fred, the Serial Innovator in the medical instrumentation business who sought interesting problems in university laboratories and venture incubators, also described spending a day at the hospital doing nothing but following a nurse, observing her daily routine, and trying to have no preconceived ideas of why she was doing what she was doing. As she was working with patients, he would ask, "Why are you doing it that way?" Then, at the end of the day, the conversation became more focused. For example, "I saw you do this—is that what you normally do? If you didn't have to do that, what would be better?" Through observation, Serial Innovators like Fred begin to understand enough to ask useful questions about the details of customer problems and challenges.

Serial Innovators were adamant that customer engagement had to take place at the *customer location.* Just as Adam Gudat indicated that having "Muhammad go to the mountain" was important in getting project buy-in when he was recruiting team members, going to the customer's location is important for building rapport with them. One Serial Innovator went so far as to say that you had to drive yourself to the location so that you could understand the context even more completely. Another Serial Innovator prescribed that every engineer should spend at least five days in a customer facility every year. Showing customers respect by visiting them in this way allows Serial Innovators to build rapport and to learn about relevant contexts. By visiting customer facilities alone, "your senses are more attenuated," ensuring that Serial Innovators observe more clearly and listen more intently. "Seeing" the problem in the customer's location makes it more real and increases the desire to solve the problem.

In talking to customers, most engineers ask concrete "how" or "what" questions. However, these questions tend to solicit concrete answers relating what customers know, rather than what they do not know. *"Why"* questions are critical precisely because problems can be difficult to articulate. When customers are asked "why" they do things, the conversation becomes more indirect and philosophical, and root causes can become more apparent. "Why" questions also lead to mutual understanding, the third aspect of building rapport. Even in the few instances when customers seem certain about what they want, they often do not know the "why" behind their needs, and concomitantly may not be able to visualize alternative solutions. "Why" questions vary and may include: Why is it that way? Why are you doing that? Why do you think you need that (technical feature)? These questions are critical to helping customers articulate what they are trying to accomplish, versus what they think they are doing. Two more important "why" questions are: (1) Why would you buy this product? or (2) Why would you not buy the product? Asking these questions and probing the answers carefully can help customers begin to articulate what they are experiencing.

The corollary to asking good questions is being able to *listen effectively*, which also helps build trust. Listening is more involved than hearing; it includes really comprehending what is said and its root cause implications. It is more than just hearing and much harder to do. We all routinely hear what people say without listening to what they mean. Effective listening comes from being curious and wanting to understand completely, which drives a Serial Innovator to probe the underlying meanings of what is being said. This desire to delve into the underlying meanings helps both the Serial Innovator and the (potential) customer explore the problem, and this mutual understanding builds rapport. Serial Innovators have to know all of the specific details in order to understand customers and their problems completely.

Listening is a tricky process, because technologists tend to favor, a priori, certain approaches to a problem that can cloud their judgment. Biases can appear even when one takes good notes and reviews what he or she heard. Data can be distorted, essential pieces of information that are at odds with ingoing beliefs can be forgotten, and the entire experience can be contaminated. Successful understanding requires listeners to withhold their judgments and biases.

Listening involves more than just hearing the words people say, which is in part why Serial Innovators favor face-to-face interactions over those by phone or e-mail. Experienced Serial Innovators become very skilled at looking for and attending to the nuances of communication and body language. For example, they may assess how fast customers relate what they want. Do they know right away, or do they have to think about it? Quick answers may indicate an expected or standard answer, or may suggest that the customer has already reflected on the issue carefully. Only probing more deeply will tell the Serial Innovator which is the case. Along with the speed of response, body language and fluency may provide clues as to the depth to which the issues being discussed have been thought about. The way things are said is crucial, which again, is why face-to-face discussions are considerably more effective than telephone conversations or e-mail queries.

The Serial Innovator's detailed work with a small set of customers accomplishes the first level of defining and understanding a specific problem that is important to at least some customers. One Serial Innovator felt that he understood the problem when the customer said a sentence and he heard paragraphs. He understood the context, the nuances, the implications, and how the answer fit with answers from other customers.

As described in Chapter 2, these tasks are not completed in a strict linear fashion, but rather in an interactive and iterative attempt to find and understand an interesting and important problem. A more complete understanding of the problem also involves understanding the market and the competitors in ways that enable the Serial Innovator to invent and create.

CUSTOMERS TO MARKETS — COMPLETING
THE UNDERSTANDING

While studying individual customer problems, Serial Innovators also work long and hard to understand the marketplace in aggregate, obtaining inputs from multiple sources to do so. Serial Innovators view the market as consumers voting with their pocketbooks. Aggregate market information tells them something about the context of the current mind-set of people. It indicates what customers are doing; Serial Innovators interpret what those behaviors mean and how that information can be applied to product development. Serial Innovators see potential in sources of data that other people don't pay attention to in research and development (R&D).

Serial Innovators dive into quantitative data, studying the market in aggregate to help find interesting problems that matter to many customers. They examine quantitative data already available to the firm in ways no one else has previously. One Serial Innovator examined years of sales data to determine correlations between customer groups and specific configurations of their products. Then they examined explicitly what those customers were doing with that unique product configuration.

The most impressive story we heard about a Serial Innovator using available data to quantitatively understand a market in aggregate came from Chuck House. Although he was a lifelong nonsmoker, he had developed emphysema while working for Hewlett-Packard (HP) in Colorado. Chuck and his doctor figured that his emphysema most likely arose due to exposure to air pollution. Shortly after Chuck found out that he had this disease, Colorado's legislature assembled a task force to develop recommendations for the state's environmental laws, especially laws concerning air pollution. They were trying to determine whether the nation's highest-altitude states should have different pollution laws than lower-altitude states. Although Chuck was trained as an electrical engineer and knew nothing about air pollution, he got himself appointed to the task force, figuring he had a direct stake in the outcome because of his emphysema. The task force's approach to that point had been to see what other high-altitude states, such as Utah, had implemented, taking a "follower" approach to the situation.

Chuck, however, proposed doing a statistical study of emphysema deaths in the state, to see if they could be related to other environmental and air-quality conditions (in addition to smoking, which was already a well-known correlation). At that time, Colorado had the fourth highest emphysema rate of all of the states in the United States, and that rate had been climbing steeply for the previous fifteen years. From the data, Chuck found that only 9 out of Colorado's 62 counties (14.5%) accounted for the bulk of the 2,752 emphysema deaths of the previous decade, and none of those counties were the densely populated areas such as Denver. Upon further investigation, he found out that each of these counties had a cement factory, refinery, or smelter that was throwing tons of pollutants into the air, which also were remaining in the air, trapped in local inversions. The emphysema rates in these counties were up to 15 times the national emphysema rates, contributing heavily to Colorado's average of 1.3 times the national rate. Previous regulation had focused on air quality of densely populated areas, like Denver, assuming that these areas would require the highest levels of regulation. However, based on Chuck's findings, the legislature turned its focus to legislation for plants operating in rural areas. These data all were publicly available. Serial Innovators use this kind of analysis of available data to understand the market in aggregate and to determine whether a particular customer problem generalizes to the market overall.

Serial Innovators also strive to understand how competitors have addressed customer needs. A rigorous examination of competitors' products and services is a critical part of the knowledge base Serial Innovators build to gain insight into customer requirements. Remember that Jim bought and tore down every brand of laptop available in the market as part of his investigation of the problem of LCD screens and laptop power management. Another Serial Innovator examined all the brands for his product category in the market to determine what they had in common. He looked not just at brand trends but also at form trends, size trends, and other relevant characteristics. This investigation revealed market trends that had occurred over time but that no one else had identified. He also gained insights into which products were successful under which specific conditions. Another Serial Innovator created a description of the leadership team of every competing product. He made the effort to meet the key business manager, the lead technical person, and the marketing person of every competing product in an effort to "size up the competition." He observed, "If you are going to run the race, you had better understand your competitors." He was in the race for the long term, committed to winning.

Many Serial Innovators were proud of their competitor knowledge, as typified by comments like: "I am very familiar with all aspects of the current products that address these problems," or "I have knowledge of the whole business and understand the marketplace." Although these types of comments can sound self-serving and arrogant, when probed, these Serial Innovators really did have deep competitive knowledge. Just as the technical knowledge of Serial Innovators is broader and deeper than most, so is their knowledge of the competition and the market.

Additional knowledge is gained by reading the periodicals related to their target markets. Sometimes they attend conferences to learn. One Serial Innovator went to six or seven conferences a year to see the big trends. He spent time working the convention floor, asking what was special and interesting about different technologies and products. Another Serial In-novator described visiting suppliers from different industries, mining pat-ent databases for peripheral industries, and attending their trade shows to get exposure to ancillary industries and technologies. As was described in Chapter 2, Innovators look broadly into analogous domains to find po-tential breakthrough solutions.

Serial Innovators' knowledge of competitors and customers is deep and well grounded. Having customer understanding and being able to speak clearly and powerfully about what the customers want give Serial Innovators credibility, managerial support, and, subsequently, considerable power in their organizations. Speaking with firsthand customer knowledge and sup-porting statements with customer testimonials gain Serial Innovators cred-ibility and management support. Intimate and detailed customer knowledge is a necessary tool when dealing with organizational politics and in trying to convince others of the viability of the new product concept (Chapter 4).

Although we have focused so far on Serial Innovators' efforts to un-derstand customers and markets, they do not do this work alone. Other members of R&D and people from other functions join the "team" to gather information, learn, and help create the products. One Serial Inno-vator convinced his company to send him, along with a marketing person and a strategic analyst, on a "world tour," just talking to a wide range of customers and potential customers to get a sense of the worldwide market for the proposed product concept. This tour resulted in confirmation of the product concept and agreement on the top five "great problems" that still needed to be addressed.

Because the market space for a breakthrough innovation is new to an organization and so little is known about it, predicting demand is a very difficult task. Having someone from marketing, in particular, help with this task and with building the initial sales estimate can prove valuable. The difficulty of building these estimates signals the importance of data quality.

Data quality and validity both matter to Serial Innovators: "You can only be an innovator if you have data, and you're only as good as the quality of the data you have." Serial Innovators are particularly careful to check the validity of the data they gather. Only once they are convinced that their data are valid and as high quality as possible do they then use those data to reinforce the current worldview, challenge the thinking of others, or create a new paradigm altogether.

Often, Serial Innovators' views counter prevailing opinions and challenge long-held assumptions and beliefs. They find that a consensus does not make an assumption true. They find data, check the validity of the data, and then use the data to challenge prejudices and to tell a different story. Direct customer input is a powerful data source that is highly valued in a firm. When Serial Innovators can say, "This is what the customers are saying and these are the implications," these powerful data and the resulting logical argumentation can lead to greater organizational acceptance.

CREATING THE SOLUTION

The Serial Innovator's ultimate goal is to create a new product that fundamentally transforms the product category. Building on their in-depth customer analysis and broader market examination, Serial Innovators and their teams are now poised to innovate and to build the products that will solve the problems identified. Because they already have had extensive customer contact, Serial Innovators have likely found "customers of difference" who can work with the teams to wrestle with product concept definitions and help move productively toward solutions.

A common perception is that you get significantly out-of-the-box thinking from people who have not been involved with customers and their products, as they are not constrained by assumptions based on "what is." In our experience, that is just flat-out wrong. People who do not understand the customer's total system can provide novel ideas, but the odds that those ideas are practical and useful are minimal. The people who come up with good ideas are those who understand the entire customer system well, because they understand both its limitations and its opportunities for improvement—they *discern* what "could" be possible.

The acts of discovery, of "coming to know," of being able to discern described by Serial Innovators exhibit a pattern of knowing first articulated by Polanyi (1966).* To "come to know" and understand deeply,

---

* For a more complete explanation of "knowing" as it relates to Serial Innovators, please see Vojak et al. (2010). Also see Meek (2003) for an explanation of knowing and seeing.

Serial Innovators live their problems; they *indwell*, immersing themselves totally in countless details about customers, markets, competitors, technologies, manufacturing processes, finance, colleagues, senior management, etc. However, although Serial Innovators are keenly *aware* of these details (called *subsidiary awareness*), they do not *focus* on them and try to produce a solution for each detail. Instead, they focus on potential solutions that simultaneously and holistically address the complete array of constraints and customer needs, called *focal awareness*.

The process of simultaneous subsidiary and focal awareness is similar to what happens when people view Random Dot Stereograms, such as those found in the *Magic Eyes* (N.E. Thing Enterprises 1993) children's books (Meek 2003). By "looking beyond" the mass of randomly spaced individual dots in these figures, a picture of some specific object appears. In the same manner, Serial Innovators "look beyond" the wealth of details they have acquired through indwelling to arrive holistically at potential solutions. This process accounts for the considerable time that breakthrough innovation typically requires. The deep understanding acquired in the act of *indwelling* is not possible without significant investment of oneself over an extended period of time.

One Serial Innovator lived with his problem to such an extreme that he was thinking about it all the time. At night, he decided what he wanted to think about just before he went to bed. "For the last four months I would say, 70% of the mornings between two and three I'll wake up with some important part of it." His mind was always actively on this problem. When he went on vacation, he took the project along rather than a book or other form of entertainment. He was continually engaged in the project and tied everything he saw or did back to it. "My wife dragged me to some plantations in Georgia. The last thing I care about is that. But seeing all those trees gave me the insight that I could display a lot of the work I'm doing as a tree." These are the behaviors and actions associated with "indwelling," that is, with living the problem.

Tom Osborn also indwelled. As shown in the Introduction, he personally examined hundreds of used feminine hygiene pads, he talked in depth with friends and family about their experiences in testing the prototypes he created, and he engaged the services of medical models to provide him with even more intimate details about the process of menstruation. He even pursued this investigation in spite of the threat of being dismissed for doing so. His relentless search for detailed information finally led him to be able to reframe the fluid capture problem to one of comfort, and, in turn, to develop the Always® Ultra.

CUSTOMER ENGAGEMENT DURING DEVELOPMENT
Once a potential solution has been created and a product concept exists, customer engagement and feedback become even more critical to fine-tune the solution into a commercial success. The skills of asking good questions and listening carefully continue to apply, but they are complemented by additional skills needed to present the concept/prototype and to engage the customer in problem solving. In this task, Serial Innovators frequently think ahead of the development process. For example, one team was working toward a quantitative concept test, where the product idea or concept is presented to consumers and they indicate how interested they are in buying it. The Serial Innovator's question to the team was, "Well, what really are we going to learn from the concept test? What if we assume the consumer response is this [very high] number? What else is going to affect the viability of this project?" That question helped the team see that success did not just depend upon customer acceptance. In this case, it led them to broaden the inquiry. Consumer response was not an obstacle; it was really the distribution system that could determine whether the product could succeed.

Concept and prototype testing may involve a lengthy conversation that gets to the details by *eliciting trade-offs* the customer would be willing to make. Here, Serial Innovators find customers willing to engage in a "game," where the Serial Innovator gets them to make a series of trade-offs about the features of the product. For example, the Serial Innovator may ask: "Suppose I could give you this performance point but then took away this other one. Which would you prefer? Well, what if that raised the price by X amount?" Customers making these types of trade-offs provide a sense of how negotiable a feature is and how interdependent it is with other features. In product categories with a large number of potential customers, this type of trade-off analysis may be performed using a formally executed large-sample quantitative market research project, or "conjoint analysis." However, because of the nature of breakthrough products, large-sample market research typically is not possible. Thus, Serial Innovators use this more qualitative version of trade-off analysis that focuses on discussion and understanding. Structuring the conversation and listening carefully to customer feedback enables the innovation team to learn quickly what is acceptable, what is not, and what trade-offs could be made. These interactions also prepare for the last critical part of the hourglass model of innovation—creating market acceptance.

Although many firms use techniques similar to these during development, Serial Innovators reach out more frequently. Additionally, the information they seek is more diagnostic in nature than predictive. Much of the market research done during development for more incremental products aims to help firms predict sales levels given a marketing plan. However, Serial Innovators use concept and prototype tests more qualitatively to probe for aspects of the customers' needs that still are not being met and aspects of the product solution that are technically inelegant or not intuitive to use—and to ensure that they still understand how the solution will fit into the marketplace.

CREATE MARKET ACCEPTANCE

Just because a potential solution has been found does not mean that customer engagement is complete. A Serial Innovator is satisfied only when the products he or she creates are in the customers' hands and solving their problems. Continued customer engagement also enables them to identify the next set of product improvements that will capture even more of the market.

Through concept and prototype testing during development, the team already has created market acceptance with a few key customers. The challenge now is to create that acceptance with other customers and with potential customers. Serial Innovators' previous in-depth work has given them intimate knowledge about gaining customer acceptance.

Serial Innovators realize that product or marketing adjustments eventually may be required. For example, one Serial Innovator thought she had created an antiaging ointment, which she planned to package in a tube. However, once the product was developed, she learned that, to the customer, it was neither a cream nor a lotion but the best of both. They thus repackaged the product in a small pump jar that communicated to customers that it was a different type of product. The product itself did not change through this phase of customer engagement; she learned how to most appropriately present, position, and package the product.

By working with the marketing function at this stage, Serial Innovators can participate in building more creative and innovative marketing plans. Serial Innovators can influence marketing plans because they have deep knowledge of the consumers' concerns, perspectives, and biases. For example, in feminine hygiene pads, where absorption and fluid capture was critical and the new Always Ultra product was thinner than previous products, marketing was unsure how to overcome the consumer bias that "thicker is better." Tom Osborn came up with a series of clever demonstrations showing that the thick materials were more likely to leak than the thin materials in several situations. Marketing, without Tom's combined technical and customer use knowledge, could not have developed these demonstrations, which ultimately were included in the advertising campaign and were highly effective in overcoming customer bias.

Seminars and workshops are powerful ways to teach customers about a new product: how it is different and how they can put it into use. Many Serial Innovators, including the example of Mark in the food oils business presented in Chapter 2, gave examples of creating workshops and seminars to help promote their products. Mark had used a customer request to learn more about using emulsifiers in food products as a way to introduce his company's new class of protein emulsifiers to them. "So we brought in our emulsifier expert and spent about twenty minutes on traditional emulsifier technology and lipid systems, then turned the rest over to this guy who had a great deal of experience using proteins as emulsifiers in food systems. Putting the right person with the right product in front of the customer solved their problems and quite a bit of sales came out of it." Another Serial Innovator even worked with a professor to write a book to explain how to use the new product, which gave the product credibility with the technical user community.

Selling directly to customers enables the Serial Innovator to understand the product's strengths and liabilities and then to use that information in the next generation of products. Rarely does the first product solve all of the customer problems and capture the entire market, but it does provide significant clues as to potentially useful future modifications. Serial Innovators are always looking for what else can be done to better solve customer problems or solve more of them simultaneously.

One Serial Innovator described his firm's effort to expand the problems solved using baby diapers as an example. Initially, paper-based diapers were just a replacement product for cloth diapers, a convenience product for parents and care providers. Then they were sold as "helping your baby develop by getting a good night's sleep," because urine was wicked away from skin contact through a dry-feeling top sheet. Then they were sold as "helping children learn how to dress" through their pull-up form. And now they also are sold as ways to "help the child learn colors and numbers" through the designs and patterns printed on them. The problems that the product category solves keep expanding.

SUMMARY

Serial Innovators begin and end with a customer focus. Everything they do centers on understanding and solving customer problems. Customers are the source of potential problems, and they are integral to problem definition, framing the solution, final product delivery, and sales. Knowing how to engage with customers, learn from them, and satisfy them are critical skills every Serial Innovator needs to develop as early in their career as possible and continuously hone over time.

Lessons for Serial Innovators

Do It Yourself.   Customer understanding comes from a do-it-yourself (DIY) needs gathering process. Marketing is not the answer—in none of our cases did customer understanding, problem definition, or product specifications come from marketing's input. Marketing staff members are neither the bad guys, nor are they stupid; they can offer some useful data. However, the more time, distance, and different perspectives there are between you and the source of the information (customers) you need, the greater the likelihood of distortion and misunderstanding. So Serial Innovators practice DIY market research.

Go to the Customer.   You will learn more by being at the customer site, observing individuals experiencing problems in their own environment, understanding the context of the situation, and exploring interest points that may be peripheral to the primary target, but that may ultimately impact the viability of a potential solution—seeing firsthand what the problems are. If you see it, you have a chance to understand it more deeply.

Ask and Listen.   Be curious and understanding. Be the student and let the customer be the professor. Asking good questions, especially "why" questions, leads to deeper disclosure from the customer and, thus, to a better understanding of both problem and solution. Listening while suspending judgment enables you to hear what is being said, place that information in a useful context, and understand the problems at a deep fundamental level.

Understanding Takes Time.   Understanding customers, really understanding, and bringing them to a mutual understanding, takes time and effort. It is not a process that can be hurried. It takes time to absorb, reflect, and then understand. Prematurely moving to closure on a concept undermines understanding and the probability of a creating a breakthrough.

Personal Commitment.   Understanding customers' problems requires deep personal commitment to live with, wrestle with, and dwell with those problems until they become yours. They require immersion. As those problems become yours to solve, your intrinsic motivation to explore, research, understand, and create increases. Serial Innovators cannot innovate in a product category they do not "like."

The Power of Customer Data.   Customer data are powerful in convincing others in your organization to take the actions you suggest. Technical data are essential and part of the solution. However, persuasive customer data move people and allow you to speak confidently and authoritatively. Customer support for a breakthrough concept is extremely powerful in getting organizational action as we will see in Chapter 4.

Stay with the Product.   There is much to be learned from customers in the project's late stages and even after initial commercialization. This information can help create customer acceptance and define the next generation of products. In a breakthrough product, it is extremely unlikely that everything will be understood and implemented perfectly in the first generation. Even if the initial product is nearly perfect, it will attract users who differ slightly in their needs from those targeted in the first generation of product development, as well as competitors who may approach the problem in a different way. Thus, future product evolution will be necessary. Customer reactions, feedback, and adoption data will be critical for determining future product directions.

Managerial Implications

Engineers have to be with the customers. The challenge is to make customer interactions useful and powerful early in an engineer's career so that he or she understands how to truly engage with customers, understand their problems, and collaborate with them across the project life cycle.

Be patient. Managers almost always push for closure before a problem is sufficiently understood. As a result, some engineers may not move on to invention unless pushed. So the challenge for managers is to know when and how to push for closure and progress. Part of that understanding comes from assessing the pace of learning and when understanding starts to converge on potential solutions.

Value deep customer knowledge. Use that knowledge and those data to influence the organization to give the Serial Innovators and their teams the time and space required to create breakthrough new products.

Enable engineers to stay with the project. Explore what engineers and Serial Innovators learn from staying with the project in the development and implementation phases, particularly around product introduction to customers.

4   NAVIGATING THE POLITICS
OF BREAKTHROUGH INNOVATION

For most existing companies, over 90% of the organization's resources, people, energy, and management attention are focused on producing, delivering, and improving today's products. This chapter reviews some of the political challenges associated with getting breakthrough innovations that move the firm into new white space accepted for development and describes how Serial Innovators influence their organizations to move these types of innovations into the development pipeline. We then outline the early careers of Serial Innovators and show how they decide to engage the organization. Finally, the chapter examines the "political" activities they manage during the project, particularly when stakes are high.

POLITICAL CHALLENGES OF BREAKTHROUGH INNOVATION
Managers whose priorities are optimizing today's business are focused on the competition, growing market share, sustaining margins, and improving current products—all important organizational goals that ironically may inhibit future growth through breakthrough innovation. When organizations are focused on current business and products, new breakthrough innovations almost always are seen as a distraction from today's pressing needs. This perspective can impede breakthroughs from being accepted into the development pipeline.

Breakthrough innovations compete with current product lines for resources and attention (Christensen 1997), making them politically difficult to undertake. Take the example cited in the introductory chapter, with Tom Osborn. The first-generation Always® product was successful in the marketplace. Development was engaged in producing evolutionary improvements to the pad, manufacturing had geared up and was working to increase production efficiencies, and marketing was working frantically to capitalize on the product's initial success. No one wanted to shift gears to work on a revolutionary concept that would require major changes in the development program, manufacturing process, and marketing talking points. It ultimately took the support of two senior managers who were not entrenched in the old paradigm to get Tom's Always Ultra pad concept accepted for large-scale production. Entrenched firms and managers strongly resist changes like this.

Breakthrough innovations also are politically difficult because Serial Innovators often reframe the initial problem statements presented to them. They see the problem differently from everyone else in the organization, and they likely have solved a different problem from that initially posed. Call it the Galileo scenario—the Serial Innovator looks at the same data as everyone else, but sees a very different solution. Tom Osborn also experienced this phenomenon when he saw the solution to feminine care needs differently from everyone else in his organization. By adding comfort to the current problem of protection needs, his model required a solution more like a garment than the bulky products on the market at that point in time. His views, and even fairly compelling customer feedback data, initially were not sufficient to change the minds of his managers, who were focused on reaping the largesse from existing products and evolving them for continued success.

Significant changes in product concepts and features can cause political difficulties because they frequently require making large infrastructure changes. Considerable capital is often invested in the status quo. Machines, processes, supply chains, and people's knowledge and skills are aligned with and optimized for the current products and materials. Thus, even though Tom Osborn's thin Always Ultra pad ultimately cost less to produce than the thicker Always pad, investments in the current manufacturing infrastructure also delayed the new pad's introduction. Breakthrough new products are often resisted most forcefully by the people who led the last product revolution. They already have worked hard to transform the organization once and resist another major transformation, knowing how difficult these changes are to implement.

Finally, breakthrough innovations may be politically difficult to accept by the firm because they raise questions about strategy in general. What is the product strategy over the short term? The long term? How does the proposed breakthrough innovation fit into the current strategy? Does it change the strategy, and, if so, is this "new" direction one in which the firm should move? Answering these questions often challenges senior executives and requires significant discussion, debate, and political maneuvering across the organization.

In Tom's case, the new pad did not affect strategy; it was just a better solution within the strategy. However, for a company making stents for propping open arteries, moving to a drug-eluting version has the potential to transform the company from a medical devices company to a drug company. This decision now has the potential to change the firm's strategy and must be debated among the senior management.

The political difficulties caused by breakthrough innovations generate challenging problems that cause many firms to stay focused on the status quo beyond when it may be wise or prudent (Christensen 1997). Most of the firm's technology Inventors are not prepared to deal with overcoming these organizational issues. Furthermore, they may want to avoid these political issues. Serial Innovators start to distinguish themselves from typical Inventors when they realize that, in order to develop breakthrough innovations, they must learn how to manage the political processes of the firm. "Politics" loses its negative connotation as they come to value it as a necessary mechanism for accomplishing what they want to get done.

EARLY CAREER ACTIONS

Building Trust and Networks Through Competence

Serial Innovators emerge sometime between five and fifteen years into their careers, depending on the organization's culture, structure, and size

(Vojak et al. 2006). Although they have many of the characteristics of Serial Innovators before they start their careers (e.g., personality, perspective, motivation[*]), these technically trained individuals also must demonstrate routine technical success and obtain knowledge of nontechnical domains such as business, strategy, and marketing before they can become Serial Innovators.

In most organizations, the freedom to explore—which is necessary to be able to innovate—is not given easily; it has to be earned. Gaining additional freedom generally requires a track record of technical accomplishment and excellent performance. Initial freedom to explore comes by successfully fulfilling basic assigned technical tasks more competently, creatively, and quickly than expected. For example, one Serial Innovator described his first research and development (R&D) assignment as "important, but boring." Rather than complain about the assignment, he found ways to complete it in 20% of his time and used the other 80% to explore other projects going on in R&D and gain learning about the business of his division in general.

Dave, our nut roasting Serial Innovator from Chapter 2, achieved his first significant technical success out of school when he untangled the relationships leading to achieving consistent nut roasting outcomes. Because this effort more than doubled the roaster's throughput, it allowed the plant to grow production levels while shutting down one of the firm's two roasters, significantly boosting margins without changing customer prices. This huge technical and business success allowed this engineer to acquire more freedom to explore other technical issues he encountered.

Each of our Serial Innovators demonstrated their technical competence and ability to get things done early in their careers. This high level of performance begins to give young engineers some freedom to explore the organization, to learn in domains outside of their narrow technical specialty, and to contribute to their colleagues' tasks while completing their own. Their reputation for accomplishment spreads slowly across the organization, first to engineering peers, then to management, and finally to

---

[*] See Chapter 5 for details.

people in other functions and divisions. In most instances, Serial Innovators establish themselves as reliable resources fairly early; their competence and excellent performance builds trust.

In organizations, trust builds relationships that become essential to accomplish daily tasks. I trust you and you trust me. When trust is present, I will do things for you that I wouldn't do for other people, as I know that you would do extraordinary things for me. There are four essential elements of creating trust between individuals (Williams 2001):

1. Competence—Do you have the necessary skills for the tasks at hand? For example, one young engineer was described by a technician: "When Kirk tells us to do something, it works. We can't say the same about many of his peers."

2. Reliability—Do you do what you say you will do?

3. Openness and honesty—Do you give all the facts or only those that put you in the best light? Do you volunteer information, rather than have it pulled out of you?

4. Concern—Are you considerate and do you care about others? Often, this level of concern is manifest in giving and sharing credit.

Trust between two people also builds mutual respect that allows employees to account for each other's unique talents and limitations. Many Serial Innovators described their capacity to see the abilities of other people and to engage others in ways that recognized those abilities. All workers within an organization get things done more quickly and efficiently when there is mutual respect.

This mutual respect helps Serial Innovators gain credibility with useful social networks, both inside and outside of the firm. In short, appreciating others' talents and abilities is part of building and maintaining a powerful social network, upon which Serial Innovators later can draw for help.

Every Serial Innovator we interviewed had a significant track record of technical performance, a powerful sense of trust (both engendered quickly with us and demonstrated across the organization), and a large network of knowledgeable connections both inside and outside the organization. With this foundation, established early in their careers and cultivated throughout, Serial Innovators were prepared to challenge their initially unsophisticated view of how things get done in the organization and what their role in getting them done needs to be.

The Naïve View of How Things Get Done in the Organization

Successful technology push projects need a Champion to shepherd them across the Valley of Death (Markham 2002). Champions are needed because most Inventor technologists have what Serial Innovators describe as a "naïve" view of organizational politics and influence in the firm. This naïve view is characterized by several beliefs or assumptions:

- Invention is sufficient. Inventing something new is a difficult and challenging task. Inventors believe that the beauty of their creation should be sufficient to obtain acceptance. This is the "if you build it, they will come" syndrome.

- Managers have the responsibility to recognize the value of the invention and to see that it is used effectively in the organization. Managers routinely make this link for incremental innovations, so in the technologist's mind it is reasonable to expect that managers will take this responsibility for more significant breakthrough innovations.

- If invention is sufficient for acceptance and the next steps are the responsibility of the manager, it is reasonable to conclude that nothing more is expected of the technologist after invention. The responsibility for development and commercialization passes off to "someone else."

The typical technologist has a narrow view of his or her tasks as being technical in nature. The Inventors we studied all maintained this view throughout their entire careers. The result is that many interesting technologies are invented by Inventors, and these technologies do not become manifest as commercialized products. These nonstarters raise the question, "What do Serial Innovators do differently?"

Crossing the Bridge of Political Reality

At some point in their careers, Serial Innovators realize they have to help others in their organizations understand and use the innovations they create. One Serial Innovator expressed this sentiment with an analogy to the

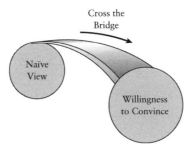

Cross the
Bridge

Naïve
View

Willingness
to Convince

FIGURE 4.1   The political maturing of innovators

proverbial tree falling in a forest: "If you create knowledge but it's never heard about, known, appreciated, used, or retained, was knowledge really created?" He realized that no one else was going to push his project through for him. He was going to have to cross the bridge and enter the political arena in his firm (Figure 4.1).

At least two factors drive Serial Innovators to this realization. The first relates to the combination of their personalities, perspectives, and motivations (see Chapter 5): because they are curious and internally motivated to solve important customer problems, they are more likely to seek inherently "interesting" problems. They pursue the hard problems that no one has been able to solve, as in Dave's nut roasting problem. Their creativity and intuition compel them to struggle with these difficult problems, to understand them deeply, and to reframe them in solvable and salable ways. However, their solutions may differ dramatically from their managers' expectations, and their managers may struggle to recognize these solutions as significant breakthroughs, as in the case of Tom Osborn. Thus, Serial Innovators have to demonstrate that their solution is better than the expected outcome to the very boss who initially assigned them their development task. Managing the political process starts with influencing their supervisor(s) to accept their solution.

Because Serial Innovators have found unique and difficult problems, no one else feels as passionately about the problem and the solution as they do. Therefore, there are few people (if any) to whom Serial Innovators can turn for guidance, support, and acceptance. Realizing that they must create their own support systems, Serial Innovators consciously decide that they have to engage the organization and become willing to convince others that their solutions are worthy of organizational support. For some, like Tom Osborn, this realization came gradually over many years of experience as he could engage with higher levels of management and could see how the political process worked. For many, the realization came in an "Aha!" moment when they noticed that their methods for moving their projects forward were not working and that they needed to try something radically different. If no action was taken proactively to influence the organization, the innovation they had created was going to die of benign neglect. And to Serial Innovators, this potential outcome is an anathema.

Serial Innovators quickly learn that they must do more than convince one person of the importance of their innovation, as may be the case in the simple view of organizational politics. One Serial Innovator described a conversation with his manager where the manager said, "You have me convinced; now you need to help me convince a larger set of other people." For virtually all breakthrough innovations, gaining acceptance for the project is a problem of convincing many people, almost all of whom are outside the Serial Innovator's personal sphere and also outside of their comfort zone. Recall that Tom Osborn had to persuade not just his managers, but his managers' managers as well as managers of parallel groups before the organization solidified behind the comfortable thin pad concept.

In another example, one Serial Innovator's "Aha!" moment came when he was pitching an idea to his chief technology officer (CTO). Although the CTO said, "I think that's an absolutely wonderful idea," he then continued on:

I can't give you the money. You've gotta go get the money from all the players. Even if I had the money, I wouldn't give it to you, right? Because you need to get their sponsorship. It's not my project, it's their project.

The Serial Innovator's reaction was:

That was an eye-opening experience. Get this—get the highest level that you think is the decision-maker and they're sending you back down the organization. . . . I was like, oh my God, instead of getting one guy to buy this now, I gotta pull the Energizer Bunny out of the hat for twenty people.

Almost all of the people who need to be convinced are outside of the R&D organization and at a significantly higher level in the organization; convincing them would pose a challenge for virtually anyone. For many Inventors, the need to convince many people is sufficient reason to passively wait for "someone else" to recognize the brilliance and potential of their innovations. Too often, these people become cynical about management and about the organization because they see inventions languish in the lab rather than make a difference to the business. Serial Innovators avoid this cynicism by accepting political interactions as part of the process of creating breakthrough innovations.

However, there are several significant implications associated with this acceptance. First, Serial Innovators realize that their primary motivation for political interaction is getting the product for which they are so passionate into the hands of customers. They are committed to deliver results in spite of whatever situations they face organizationally. Thus, they are willing to take the time to develop an understanding about the interpersonal relationships in the firm, exploring where the power lies, who really makes resourcing decisions, and who is in alliances with whom.

They also realize that there are limits to what they can achieve developmentally until they have obtained formal organizational acceptance for the project. Because of their network, they may be able to push a project along further than most people without formal acceptance. Adam Gudat, for example, knew which engineers in the company were unhappy with their assigned projects and was able to persuade them to help move his under-the-table side projects along. Nonetheless, they need their projects to be formally accepted in order to have the "big" resources needed to move forward from technical invention to concept proof and physical development. "It is not a project until it is accepted."

While pursuing formal acceptance, they come to realize that facts are necessary to gain project acceptance, but they are not sufficient. Serial Innovators have to learn to sell in a way that is congruent with their personal style. There are nearly as many different personal styles of influence as there are Serial Innovators, but they all have to learn to sell effectively. Now, beyond developing relationships with other technical experts across the organization as they already have done early in their careers, they also have to learn to develop relationships with the decision-makers in the firm. During this process, Serial Innovators come to realize that selling is incremental. The initial "sell" is almost never a "blank check" for executing the entire project. Initial acceptance is almost always a "positive pathway to begin moving forward." It allows Serial Innovators enough resources and time to take the next step forward, whether that is showing proof of concept, developing a virtual prototype, or creating the next model. At each stage, they use their small-scale accomplishments to sell the next step in the process to management. Just like entrepreneurs who have to meet certain milestones to obtain new levels of funding, Serial Innovators know that they are selling the next incremental step that will help move their projects forward.

For example, Adam Gudat at Caterpillar worked over many years, selling to many different managers, groups, and organizational units to get his company to implement full remote electronic control in their earthmoving machines. According to him, he got the firm's products to that state by starting little projects that allowed him to demonstrate what would be possible sometime in the future. An early project involved developing and installing a unit in a truck that was programmed to automatically drive around the R&D campus with no human driver. He would demonstrate one small capability, sell it to his manager, then to the business unit manager, and then to another manager from a different product line that might be able to use that capability in the future as well. From the combination of those managers, he could earn money, time, and freedom to develop the next little piece of technology that would take him one step closer to realizing his ultimate vision (dropping machines onto a mountain to build an airport with no human intercession). There is almost never just one sell opportunity and one customer group in the firm—there are many—and the influencing and selling continues throughout the life of the project.

After accepting the political realities associated with gaining formal project approvals, Serial Innovators apply themselves to learning how to influence those who will be making the decisions, just as they previously applied themselves to learning about technologies, businesses, and markets. Rather than becoming cynical about the political process, they display a positive attitude toward it, using it as a means to teach others in the organization about the importance of what they are doing.

INFLUENCING ACCEPTANCE DURING THE PROJECT

Apply a Range of Influence Methods Flexibly and with Insight
Obviously, Serial Innovators do not emerge fully formed and ready to change the organization. However, as we encountered them, they demonstrated an impressive understanding of how organizational influence, change, and politics come about as a result of four types of influence processes (Figure 4.2):

1. Engaging people in the endeavor to get participation and buy-in;

2. Positioning the project vis-à-vis the organization's strategies;

3. Using "soft" influence tactics; and

4. Using "hard" influence tactics.

Over the years, Serial Innovators build a full arsenal of tactics across these four influence processes and develop the wisdom to know when and how to use each tactic. We describe these actions and tactics in a manner that

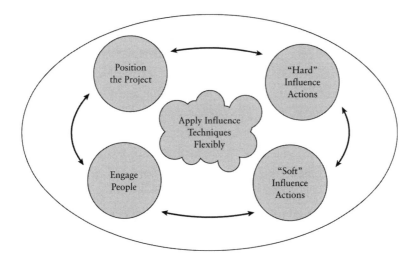

FIGURE 4.2   Influencing acceptance during the project: Applying four types of influence actions flexibly

might seem directly related to various phases of a project, but Serial Innovators applied the techniques at different times and with different goals in mind.

Engaging People: Getting Participation and Buy-In

Serial Innovators are intently selective about forming their teams. Volunteers are preferred over people assigned by management. Volunteers bring passion, enthusiasm, and they know why they are being asked to contribute. Serial Innovators look for like-minded people who are committed to the organization, hardworking, and passionate about what they do. From their networks, they know key people in different technical areas throughout the firm, what these people are doing, whether they are happy with their assignments, and what they might contribute. When Serial Innovators are able to pique the interest and stretch the capabilities of engineers, the results are amazing. Engineering team members like to contribute to projects that are challenging and potentially important; they sign on to do extra work because they get to work on something no one has done before. The engagement that comes with novel breakthrough projects, as opposed to routine incremental projects, cannot be overestimated in its power to attract volunteers from across the firm.

Whereas it is hard to get a manager to assign someone to an unapproved project, Serial Innovators persuade people to volunteer their efforts, using influence tactics to engage people to do significant extra work on their extracurricular projects—often after hours or carved out of a very busy day. Because Serial Innovators earn trust by showing concern for others, valuing others' capabilities, and sharing credit, they are able to get people to do "real" work for them in an informal, "Skunk Works" fashion that would be impossible to accomplish more formally. Assembling the right team requires understanding what motivates potential team members, having a concrete vision about the project's value, and being persuasive. For example, because Adam Gudat knew what all the engineers were doing in the firm, he knew which engineers were unhappy on their projects and offered them opportunities to work "under the table" on a more exciting project. Similarly, by openly communicating about his ideas, Tom Osborn was able get a colleague intrigued enough about the potential for a thin pad that she was willing to help him bootleg, hand-making several hundred prototype pads.

Requests for help at this level are almost always made personally and face-to-face. The more important the task, the more important it is to talk with people directly rather than via e-mail or some less personal method. When sitting down with someone, Serial Innovators can observe if their proposal is understood, or if there is another angle that could help persuade the individual. Remember, Serial Innovators are asking colleagues for favors with only their trust and goodwill—as well as their contagious excitement about the idea—as bargaining tools. Allies are created one at a time by making direct requests and selling the potential of the project.

Once people agree to contribute, they need to know what is needed from them and how their contributions will be used. Initially, when people are engaged informally, there is a period of fuzziness during which they must gain masterful understanding of the project in its totality and of how each person's contribution fits into the overall puzzle. Team members need to see how their contributions are going to make a difference in the project, and the Serial Innovator has to help them make those connections. For nonmanagement technologists, this looks and feels like a management or leadership task—and it is. Serial Innovators assume leadership responsibility for creating group ownership of their breakthrough projects. With some teams, when the strategic importance of the project is obvious, this orientation simply involves a well-run kickoff meeting where everything known about the project is shared. With other teams, more involved approaches may be required.

Frank, the heavy equipment Serial Innovator who had his team make a quilt, offers an illustrative example of this process. When developing a new type of engine to meet radically tightening emissions requirements, Frank's team was assigned to him by management, rather than hand-selected. Because of government regulations, the project had to be completed within strict parameters. If the standards were not met, the division was out of business in this product area. But at its outset, methods for meeting these regulations were technically unknown. Frank's was a very risky, must-do project.

Frank's initial assessment concluded that the team assigned to him was the "regular army" rather than the "special forces" that would have the highest probability of delivering this product. He needed his team to be fully engaged, focused, and committed; they were unaccustomed to such intense work conditions on a day-to-day basis. In his kickoff meeting, Frank did more than convey information and facilitate a discussion to achieve understanding; he provided materials and assigned each functional specialty (electronics, fuel systems, mechanical design, etc.) to build a quilt block representing that specialty's aspect of and potential contribution to the project. There was initial grumbling about "not knowing how to do this"—but that was the point. Not knowing how the team was going to be able to meet the emissions performance requirements, he thought that if he could get them working outside of their normal boxes by making a quilt, then perhaps he could do the same thing with them in designing this breakthrough engine. Not only was the project successful, but when family day came around, the engineers all proudly showed their families the quilt, which was still hanging in the department.

Serial Innovators have to learn how to engage more than just their team members and other project volunteers. Serial Innovators have to convince management, working upward in the organization to break through barriers to earn formal organizational approval. Breakthrough projects need a sponsor (someone rather high in the organization with money and perhaps other resources). Often, the sponsors may not understand the technology, but they do understand the benefits of the project to customers and to the company. It took two senior sponsors to get Tom's thin pad accepted by the organization.

Engaging a sponsor is unlike engaging a technical colleague or even a direct manager. Sponsors ask different questions and expect different answers. One Serial Innovator explained the need to translate a profound understanding into simple and straightforward explanations of the benefits to the company. He used the analogy of peacock feathers. "Managers don't care about the colors of the feathers. They don't care about the chromophores that produce those colors, the refractory indexes, and all of that. All they want to know is that it is a bird." Serial Innovators sell simply while understanding profoundly.

One mistake that Inventors may make early in their careers, as they are growing into Serial Innovators, is to be disdainful of managers who do not understand (or do not care to understand) technical details of a project. Managers pick up on negative signals, especially nonverbal negative signals such as condescending tones. Such behavior can work against gaining project acceptance. Selling simply needs to be done with respect for the positions and for the perspectives others bring. While selling to managers, Serial Innovators learn to position the product or project in the strategic context of the organization.

Position the Project
Every product commercialized needs to fit into the strategic context and goals of the organization. Sometimes how the potential breakthrough product fits with the rest of the product lines or with the company's strategy is not obvious. A key political task is thus to position the new breakthrough project so that others can understand how it fits with strategy or how it might change strategy. Positioning the product is complex and challenging, but it will determine whether or not people are able to understand why the product is important and are willing to expend energy in helping it come to fruition.

One of the techniques Serial Innovators use in positioning the project, especially when development pipelines have little or no slack in them, is to demonstrate the project's potential business value. They demonstrate that their project has greater value to the firm than one or more projects that are already under development or under consideration. However, potentially breakthrough products have uncertain returns. Thus, in addition to assembling the typical financial analyses used to demonstrate value, Serial Innovators may use other tactics, such as having customers call the project sponsor or obtaining a customer order. As one Serial Innovator said: "The best marketing research is a signed purchase order."

Knowing how to position the product depends on understanding the stakeholders and the stakes. Many of us think of just a few organizational stakeholders, such as the division president, an immediate supervisor, and the shareholders; Serial Innovators take this analysis much further. As one Serial Innovator said: "I go through the exercise of well, who are they, one by one, name by name, what do they need? For them to win, what do I have to do?" Then, Serial Innovators work diligently to make sure that each stakeholder's desires are filled. Much of this effort again is done face-to-face.

Timing is everything. Every organization has resource constraints and a product development pipeline, sometimes already overflowing with projects to support the ongoing business. At times, it will be possible to fit something into the pipeline; it will be very difficult, if not impossible, at others. Therefore, the Serial Innovator needs to understand the strategy, the product pipeline, and the dynamics of the system. For example, because Mark, the agribusiness Serial Innovator, knew that the oils division did not have the resources to support the commercialization of the breakthrough low-absorption oil he was developing, he recommended that the nutra-ceutical group take it on. This recommendation benefited the company in total without further taxing a division going through some tough times.

At times, when the pipeline is overloaded, Serial Innovators serve their organizations better by not trying to force their projects into the formal development process. That does not mean they stop working on their projects. It means that they may have to continue on in a Skunk Works mode, flying under the radar and bootstrapping resources longer than they would prefer, and longer than ultimately would be optimal for the project. Knowing when to back off is as important as knowing when to push. Having a deep understanding of the firm's strategy helps Serial Innovators determine when the timing is right.

Soft Influence Actions
"Soft influence" means moving people to your ideas and project subtly and indirectly. Serial Innovators think in terms of years, not days or months. The essence of soft influence is patience. The major actions of soft influence are: (1) planting seeds and (2) telling stories to create a vision of possibilities.

Planting seeds involves injecting thoughts into a conversation in a non-confrontational manner so that the other person can let them sink in, reflect on them, and work said ideas into their mental schema. One Serial Inno-vator liked to do this during brainstorming sessions, which are activities designed to be nonjudgmental by nature. Planting seeds means not asserting the validity of an idea or forcing an immediate decision. A more forceful approach elicits preconceived views, rather than open-minded reflection. C.K. Gunsalus, a nationally recognized colleague for her work on professionalism in academia, asks, "When was the last time you changed your mind because someone told you that your ideas were wrong or stupid?" The typical answer is never. Taking a strong position early in a discussion nearly always produces resistance and negative feelings toward the advocate of that idea or position. Even when others may eventually see that you were right, they will not want to give you that satisfaction of being right. In short, if an immediate decision is demanded, the answer almost always is no because stakeholders need time to understand the problem and the potential solution—seeds need time to germinate, grow, and mature.

Seeds also need constant attention: watering, fertilizing, and, frequently, weeding. This cultivation requires a different kind of patience. During this phase, Serial Innovators repeatedly suggest ideas, solicit and integrate feedback, and encourage people in and beyond their networks to modify or enhance the project's parameters to incorporate the project into their thinking and view of the world. By asking rather than telling, throwing out ideas at the right time, and letting others draw their own conclusions, Serial Innovators can gradually generate a robust support system. The classic perspective is that "people tolerate my conclusions, but they act on their own conclusions."

Analogies or storytelling may be necessary to the "seed-planting" process. In Chapter 2 and earlier in this chapter, we told the story of Adam Gudat trying to put global positioning systems into heavy machine equipment. Although his end vision of dropping a set of machines into a remote area to build an airport without human intervention has not yet been achieved, Adam has been able to generate enthusiasm over long periods of time as he makes incremental progress along the path to achieving it. As he told us his story of the products that had been created and delivered, it was easy to see how that vision kept him focused on long-term goals and enabled him to influence others along the way.

Soft influence actions are used by Serial Innovators over a long period of time and are applied to many different people in their extended network. Serial Innovators use influence to build organizational under-standing of their goals.

Hard Influence Actions
Although soft influence actions helpfully move the organization along, they are slow. Thus, whenever possible, Serial Innovators also use "hard influence" actions to obtain organizational acceptance for a project more quickly. Hard influence actions include using data to obtain acceptance of one's position, small proof-of-concept projects, and demonstrations of customer support.

Chuck House's exploration of emphysema required hard data to in-fluence actions. Recall that Chuck was the youngest person appointed to the Colorado committee to study air pollution. He also was the least well credentialed, having no advanced degree, whereas the others on the com-mittee were doctors, university professors, and other experts in the fields of medicine, the environment, and pollution. Alone, he would never be able to persuade the committee to take any particular action. He took charge of gathering data and figuring out how to analyze it, and he pushed the committee to base their recommendations on real data. By presenting his facts and hard data to the committee, he was able to get them to talk to each other based on what the data said was happening, rather than based on what they "knew" from their anecdotal experience. The result was a shifting of focus from just high-density geographies to "high-polluter" areas, especially those with a propensity for suffering from inversions.

The impact of prototype visualizations and demonstrations are widely recognized in new product development (NPD). The ability to see the prod-uct, to understand its structure and uses, and to get it in front of potential customers is critical for the success of breakthrough new products. Re-member how Adam Gudat used a simulation of remote machine operation to help mining companies determine what tasks would be most useful to develop remote capabilities to perform. Serial Innovators frequently use visualization software to allow others in the firm and customers to "see" a product concept before one can be built, and then develop physical prototypes, even nonfunctional ones, to get something concrete into the hands of customers sooner rather than later. Visualizing a product is vastly superior to describing verbally what might be. Even more powerful is the ability to interact with a prototype, even one that is not fully functional.

Most breakthrough products require much longer time periods for development than the traditional one- to three-year perspective of most managers and organizations. Demonstrating some small piece of the overall breakthrough will help elicit and sustain managerial interest in moving the vision forward. Demonstrations may not communicate the entire scope of a Serial Innovator's project, but they help convince management of a project's practicability and potential worth. In the early demonstration of small projects, it is thus important to say more than "look at this cool technology." A demonstration needs to provoke thought "about what this will do for customers sometime in the future." It has to prove "why" this particular piece technology or feature development is important.

Serial Innovators start small with projects that allow them to demonstrate one facet of a larger aim. If they can get someone to finance it, great. If they cannot, they do it on their own, bootstrapping the resources they need. Remember how Tom Osborn at Procter & Gamble (P&G) prototyped by hand very small batches of the new garment-style feminine hygiene pads he envisioned, and tested them with family and friend volunteers. With very little investment, he was able to start bringing new objective information back into the company and to diffuse it across the organization.

Based on a small sample set that showed directionality, but not statistical significance, Tom was able to obtain a bit more funding, which allowed him to produce larger batches of prototypes and to test them in product panels with a larger population of women, finding that women significantly preferred his prototype over the existing product. That statistically significant finding helped convince management to alter their paradigm for feminine products. Radical conclusions supported by thoughtful models coupled with powerful data and logic can trump organizational hierarchy and power to gain acceptance for projects. Serial Innovators typically have these types of hard data because they run detailed experiments testing their models of how things work. Because they understand the underlying problem more deeply than others in the organization, they can make powerful arguments for how the project should move forward and then support those arguments with data.

Finally, several Serial Innovators in our study used well-placed managers in customer organizations to influence their own management. Phone calls from influential customers to executives can significantly impact organizational decisions. For example, Sam, a Serial Innovator whose management had shut down the breakthrough electronic device project he had been working on for a year as they did not see him making "sufficient" headway, took to the street and visited three potential customers, describing his vision for how to solve the design problem they all had and presenting them with the success to date. When each in turn asked when they could expect the device to become available, he theatrically sighed and told them that he was very sorry, but management had stopped the project. "But perhaps if you called the president of the division, we could get it restarted sometime in the future." Three phone calls later, the president told Sam's manager to restart the project. To make customer pull-through work, Serial Innovators have to be strongly integrated with customers and their most important problems (as was discussed in Chapter 3).

Flexible Application of Influence Methods with Discernment and Insight

Once Serial Innovators "cross the bridge" and become willing to engage the organization politically, they use their intelligence, curiosity, and creativity to become students of people and organizations, as they have been students of technologies, markets, and businesses. Serial Innovators' political skills are not fully formed as they "cross the bridge," but when they do cross they engage fully in the political processes, and then they learn quickly. They demonstrate an unexpected level of insight and capabilities in influencing organizations, rivaling many of the best managers we have seen. They display a wide range of influence behaviors and describe how they used those behaviors flexibly and creatively to achieve their goals.

Just as Serial Innovators worked hard to understand the customer problems, they listen to managers and try to understand things from management's point of view. They would see various positions and then try to understand why people think and feel the way they do. When Serial Innovators understand the positions taken by others and the reasons for those positions, then they believe they are able to craft a solution that addresses the concerns. At every stage, Serial Innovators are making connections, really understanding others' perspectives, and being extremely creative. One Serial Innovator created a monthly newsletter that addressed organizational issues in a very creative manner, developing stylized caricatures of people from different functions and weaving them into stories that each had a moral about creating successful business situations and overcoming negative political situations in firms. Another Serial Innovator analyzed the different types of people in the audience he would be working to convince. He concluded that there were two groups: "One group doesn't believe the vision is right and the other group believes it is too difficult to achieve." The Serial Innovator then developed different strategies tailored to each group. With the former, he linked back to the customer understanding they had developed to show why it was the right thing to do. With the latter, he "painted the road map and gave them the steps that would be taken" to accomplish the tasks, showing them an incremental path that would get them to the end point.

Iterate

Serial Innovators are not so wise or competent that they always get it right the first time. However, like Tom Osborn, they do not accept no for an answer, and they keep pushing at the organization until they accomplish their goals. They learn quickly about the types of influence actions they can take and they iterate from one to another over time, depending upon which type of action seems to be more effective in the particular situation. And they persist. They work to understand the challenges of the business and then focus on solving the real problems and gaining support. As they address these complex challenges, they engage with people, learn new insights, incorporate new data, and modify their propositions until they are acceptable to the organization. Serial Innovators come to understand the stakeholders and mold their influence efforts to the needs of the people they are trying to affect.

SERIAL INNOVATORS PLAY FOR HIGH STAKES

The methods and processes described so far are reasonable approaches to dealing with the politics of getting a breakthrough innovation accepted in an organization. Sometimes, however, the rational approaches are not sufficient, and Serial Innovators push the boundaries of organizationally accepted norms and behavior to gain or retain project acceptance. They do not undertake high-personal-risk actions rashly, without thought and assessment of those risks. But to a Serial Innovator, there are times when the potential customer and organizational benefits of pushing a project far outweigh the personal risks of violating organizational norms.

Know When to Break the Rules

Organizations, especially large, mature firms, have rules about which tasks belong to which functions, and the roles different types of people in the organization are expected to fulfill. However, within every organization there is some white space that is not covered by rules and job descriptions. Serial Innovators operate much of the time within that white space. When one manager we talked to was describing two Serial Innovators as people who operated outside the box, his colleague chimed in that one of the Serial Innovators "did not even know there was a box." Working on projects that are not formally approved, getting people with other "real" jobs to join them, engaging customers without involving marketing or sales, or getting product prototypes built are just some of the day-to-day ways Serial Innovators push the organization's boundaries. At times, they even go beyond organizational norms by engaging upper-level managers before some lower-level managers have bought into the project—they jump organizational levels.

Serial Innovators can break these "small" rules on an ongoing basis because they previously have succeeded in innovating and have found managers who understand how to help protect them from organizational norms that inhibit their progress (see Chapter 7 for more). However, sometimes Serial Innovators go beyond even what their managers can protect them from.

Risk Getting Fired

Serial Innovators are willing to risk getting fired for the ideas and products they believe in. Almost half of the Serial Innovators in one firm had put their jobs on the line at least once in their careers over important breakthrough product ideas. Like Tom Osborn, some actually had been in termination discussions at the companies where they later created significant breakthrough products. As we indicated in the Introduction, HP's president even created the "Medal of Defiance," which he awarded to Chuck House as a reminder to all in the firm that breaking the rules can be associated with great reward.

The risks associated with being a Serial Innovator are real, but many of our Serial Innovators described them as being "calculated risks." They felt that the risk of doing nothing was greater than the risk of continuing down the path they were on. These are not reckless people; they are passionate people with great resolve.

SUMMARY

Serial Innovators describe themselves as consciously "crossing the bridge" from having a naïve view of the organization's political machinations to becoming willing to engage the organization politically using their talent, creativity, and persistence. Their political influencing actions emanate from a foundation of trust and respect, which must be built over time and across people in multiple functions at multiple levels of the organization. Trust and respect must be present before the actions to create breakthrough new products are undertaken. Then they learn and apply a wide variety of influence actions to help move the organization down the path to accept and support the breakthrough project. They actively engage people across the organization. They position the product and the project in the context of the organization in a way that others can see the value and benefits. Then, they use both soft and hard influence actions to help move others with them. Politics becomes an almost natural part of what they do in order to ensure that their innovations reach the market and address the customer needs they so thoroughly understand and desire to fulfill.

5   CHARACTERISTICS OF
SERIAL INNOVATORS

What makes someone willing to tackle seemingly impossible problems and to stay engaged with them over several years as the understanding of customers and technology comes together to allow them to create a break-through new product? Why would someone struggle against an organizational culture that doesn't seem to see the value of their contributions and, in fact, may actively try to suppress their contributions? How can someone delay personal gratification for several years until the final product comes to market and customers are thrilled with the results? These are just a few of the questions we asked as we wondered about the makeup of Serial Innovators. We wanted to know what made them tick and what prepared them to face the customer, technical, organizational, and personal challenges they found in bringing breakthrough new products to market over and over again. An early survey revealed that Serial Innovators emerge at between five and fifteen years of experience within a given organization. They seem to number somewhere between one out of fifty to one out of two hundred for research and development (R&D) and engineering staff, where those ratios vary depending on the size of the company—smaller companies have a higher ratio of Serial Innovators and larger companies have a smaller ratio. In fact, we estimate that the range is closer to one in five hundred in most very large (Fortune 200) companies. There are two primary reasons for Serial Innovators' relatively small numbers:

1. Their unique sets of skills and capabilities exist in only a small number of people.

2. Organizations are sometimes unable to use the talents of those who in fact do have those skills (Christensen 1997).

In sum, Serial Innovators are few and far between because breakthrough innovation talent is rare *and* it is challenging for organizations to accept Serial Innovators and what they create. Indeed, companies can be so focused on current product lines and short-term growth that they become unwilling or unable to invest in people who can provide them with new products or product lines that would move them into new white space in the longer term.

Many companies do not have the absorptive capacity to bring a large number of significantly new products to market. Companies have limited R&D budgets and, hence, the number of Serial Innovators they can support is limited, simply because having too many could overwhelm manufacturing and marketing capabilities for new products. Given the difficulty of identifying, recruiting, developing, and managing employees who challenge the organization, the product lines, and the basic assumptions held by many managers in the company, many organizations find it difficult to accept Serial Innovators. Barney Oliver, the iconoclast leader of HP Labs, once quipped: "How many geniuses will you have in a company of ten? The answer was one. In a company of one hundred? The answer was two. In a company of one thousand? The pattern is clear—three. In a company of ten thousand? The answer was zero instead of four—all of the geniuses and innovators would be driven out of the larger company." Fundamentally, Serial Innovators are sparse in large firms because of the absolute rarity in the technical population of the combination of characteristics and capabilities necessary to support breakthrough innovation. This chapter explicates those sets of characteristics that separate Serial Innovators from other technical staff members. Chapters 6 and 7 will elaborate on how to find, develop, and manage these rare employees.

THE MP⁵ MODEL: CHARACTERISTICS AND
CAPABILITIES OF THE INNER CIRCLE

We already have discussed the outer circles of process (Chapters 2 and 3) and politics (Chapter 4) of the MP⁵ model, shown in Chapter 1. This chapter focuses on the inner circle that includes: personality, perspective, and motivation, which power Serial Innovators' efforts to innovate (Figure 5.1).

Personality is the relatively stable part of the Serial Innovator—the aspect that is least likely to change over time. Serial Innovators exhibit the personality characteristics of curiosity, intuition, creativity, and systems thinking, which enables them to invent novel technologies and processes. A second set of personality variables we found included independence, confidence, and perseverance, which are important for staying with a project over an extended period of time.

Perspective is the lens through which Serial Innovators perceive the world. Perspectives, or worldviews, are formed early in life and early in a career, usually through major events or experiences that become part of the person. Serial Innovators are distinguished by what they value, what they try to do, and how they do it. In short, Serial Innovators

1. Value the common good, looking beyond themselves to consider what is good for the customer, the company, and the team;

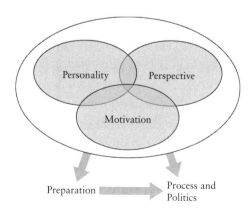

FIGURE 5.1   How personality, perspective, and motivation combine to influence preparation, process, and politics

2. Use technology as a means to make money; and

3. Seek tangible results through making connections, seeing the whole system, and seeking simplicity.

These perspectives act as guiding principles that inform Serial Innovators' daily actions and practice.

Motivation plays a central role in this capabilities model, because intrinsic motivation—strongly associated with achieving autonomy, mastery, and purpose (Pink 2009)—fuels so much of Serial Innovators' everyday behaviors. Serial Innovators are motivated by their own curiosity for solving problems, the mastery of technical fields, the joy of new discovery, and the intrinsic reward of creating something new that makes a difference in other people's lives. These factors inspire Serial Innovators to pursue new endeavors and sustain them over time as they face technical and organizational obstacles. Such enthusiastic, genuine, and contagious motivation encourages other people to share in the Serial Innovator's vision.

Crucially, these three characteristics influence and interact with each other. In fact, scholarship has struggled to differentiate between personality and motivation, particularly at the highly intrinsic side of motivation (Deci and Ryan 1985). Some academics even argue that personality and intrinsic motivation are really two sides of the same coin (Barton 2009). Partially intrinsic, motivation can be significantly impacted by extrinsic factors such as organizational culture and managerial (in)capabilities. Personality, on the other hand, is nearly immutable. Perspective is formed in a third way, through early experiences. Although it may change later in one's career, it changes only slowly over time or through major transforming experiences. Thus, although these characteristics overlap, we found clear distinctions between them as well. Personality, perspective, and motivation interact and combine to form an integrated description of who a Serial Innovator is; these factors elucidate why Serial Innovators will go to such lengths to learn and *prepare* to innovate (Figure 5.1).

When starting down an innovation pathway, Serial Innovators determine what they *don't* know, as well as what they *do* know. Then they learn what they need to know by exploring broadly and delving deeply. Serial Innovators proactively seek information across myriad topics, ranging from customers and markets to competitors, from general business knowledge to specific information about the firm's strategy and business capabilities. They obtain this information primarily through self-directed learning by observation and/or self-study, while also acquiring the technical information from whatever domain looks to be appropriate to combine with their specializations. If there is something Serial Innovators need to know, they learn it, no matter how far afield it may seem from their original backgrounds and training. The remainder of the chapter describes these Serial Innovator characteristics in depth, investigates how these characteristics interact with and reinforce each other, and, finally, suggests how these characteristics affect a Serial Innovator's development process and approach to organizational politics.

PERSONALITY CHARACTERISTICS THAT SUPPORT PROBLEM FINDING AND UNDERSTANDING

In the nature versus nurture debate, the characteristics associated with personality are those that align most closely with nature—Serial Innovators' hard wiring. As we will discuss in Chapter 6, these are the characteristics managers might use if seeking to hire potential Serial Innovators, because these qualities tend to be inherent rather than cultivated.

Curiosity is the first among these innate characteristics. Serial Innovators are natural-born inquisitors; they inherently need to understand "why." Over and over Serial Innovators described their love of mysteries and puzzles—their love of knowing why. For example, Bill Hewlett was once described as "one of the most inquisitive people I ever met. . . . When I look out the window, I'd see a tree. But he'd want to know what kind of tree it was, how it worked, what was its genesis—and he was that way whether it was art or music, or botany or electronics. That was the seed that was planted inside HP. Hewlett was the guy who gave the invention DNA to HP" (House and Price 2009, 12).

Curious people are sometimes identified by their breadth of interests; they appear to flit among ideas. However, curiosity in Serial Innovators includes two elements: (1) a broad range of interests and (2) an ability to dive deeply once those interests are piqued (Kashdan et al. 2004). On the one hand, they read more (and more broadly) than other technologists and have a wider range of outside interests. On the other hand, they often analyze more data in greater depth than their colleagues because of their desire to understand. For example, Bruce, a consumer products Serial Innovator, started new projects by taking previously completed customer focus group data and pouring over them until he knew more about customers' views than anyone else. When asked why he would analyze so much data, he responded, "How else would you know?" Serial Innovators' efforts lead toward developing a wide and deep range of ideas, concepts, and data points that provide fodder for potential solutions to problems. Their ability to probe deeply is just as remarkable as their breadth of interests.

Sometimes, Serial Innovators begin an investigation out of intellectual curiosity, wanting to know an answer just for an answer's sake. Even in these situations, their efforts quickly evolve into a more powerful and compelling desire that will improve their business. For example, Dave started off just being intellectually curious about the nut roasting problem that everyone considered an art—only the best operators could adjust the process speed, material bed depth, pressure, airflow rate, and temperature that was needed to adjust for the moisture content of the input materials. The process was almost impossible to control and the results were unpredictable—everyone saw it as the "magical art" of the roaster operator. Dave was not assigned to this project; he just thought there "should" be a better answer. He ran several experiments using the latest quality-improvement techniques, worked with a statistician on the results, and still found no answer. Then, he "happened" to take a seminar on fluid bed catalysis in the oil industry that introduced him to the heat exchange models from which he ultimately found the simple set of equations that governed roasting consistency. He then took his "curiosity" a step further and applied the solution to the true business problem, discovering that the plant had more than sufficient roasting capacity to produce all the product demanded by consumers, which also was contrary to prior beliefs. In retrospect, Dave described this investigation as becoming a "passion" that actually was much stronger than mere curiosity. He described it as a "rage against ignorance . . . I can't accept the fact that as an engineer we were just ignorant of the magic in that box." Curiosity becomes compulsion;

Serial Innovators cannot be satisfied with ignorance or explanations that lack rigor. The mystery has to be solved, and then the business has to be improved based on that new knowledge.

Intuition is an informed or expert understanding of something based on experience, deep knowledge in a domain, and a keen sense of what "might happen." Through experience-based intuition, a Serial Innovator develops hunches about what ideas to pursue. One Serial Innovator described this as a "sense of knowing," where he felt the power of an idea because of the emotion attached to it and the sensory signals that came with it. He could start seeing, feeling, and thinking of various possibilities. Serial Innovators trust themselves to sense when something is a good idea or a useful approach to the problem—"it just feels right" or "it's comfortable." Trusting intuition sometimes means following an idea when other people and perhaps other data suggest that it may not be a great idea. As described in the earlier example of Dave, he just "felt" that there had to be an answer to the roasting problem because of his previous experiences with the simplicity and elegance of nature. Such intuition is not a skill generally associated with technologists. However, intuitive thinking is a critical skill when operating at the margins of technologies and bringing in creative ideas that counter the traditional processes in a company.

Serial Innovators describe themselves (and tend to be described by others) as being more creative than their peers. **Creativity** comprises a set of abilities that allow Serial Innovators to generate many ideas and to contribute from different viewpoints or domains. Curiosity, intuition, and creativity clearly are related. The more one looks for ideas in different places or more deeply in one domain, the more ideas they likely will have and the more interesting viewpoints they may bring to the table. Creative people generate ideas profusely, and then sort through them for appropriateness in a fairly quick manner.

One technique that Serial Innovators use to generate more ideas is to suspend feasibility. For most of us, the a priori logic of a situation and our tendencies for linear logical thinking tend to constrain the potential solutions we consider. However, Serial Innovators "daydream" about what the ultimate solution could be without worrying about how to get there. Suspending judgments enables them to construct an ideal solution with the key supporting elements and then to determine which constraints can be relaxed to create a viable solution.

In addition to generating more ideas, Serial Innovators tend to approach problems from different viewpoints and to "reframe" or redefine the problem. Almost every Serial Innovator did some type of reframing to approach a problem from a new angle, which enabled them to create an unconventional solution. Recall Tom Osborn, who was in an organization that was almost completely staffed by engineers, but who conceptually transformed the technical model of feminine hygiene as the engineering problem of fluid capture into a human factors problem: "How does the body interact with these devices?" This transition opened a number of potential solution pathways that no one had been able to see previously. Seeing the problem from a totally different perspective can help create a paradigm shift, where the Serial Innovator looks at the same data as everyone else but sees an overlooked pattern. And that new pattern can help lead them to the breakthrough innovation. Creativity is part of what enables Serial Innovators to see things that others do not and then to frame issues in new ways.

Systems thinking enables Serial Innovators to integrate disparate data and information. Curiosity drives them to seek the dots for a puzzle, whereas systems thinking looks for patterns that help creatively connect the dots in logical and powerful ways. Serial Innovators look for, and expect to see, connections. They focus on "making sense" of complex situations. One Serial Innovator described the process in four steps. First, examine the entire situation and understand each of the pieces individually. Second, learn how the pieces fit together. Third, understand all of the elements well enough to change specific elements in the system to get improved results. And, finally, comprehend the system well enough to optimize the entire system rather than just one element at a time.

Serial Innovators catalog disparate ideas that they run across in their investigations into groupings of similar pieces of knowledge, and they pull those groups out and look for connections as they consider a problem. In Chapter 2, Sandra described these groupings as dust balls that she moved around in her mind. On the one hand, she was learning about the dust balls individually and trying to make each one a little bit more "solid."

Simultaneously, she was also moving them around, trying to make connections across the dust balls. If the two dust balls connected, what would that look like? Other Serial Innovators used the analogies of having ideas on fishing bobbers or on bookshelves that they revisited and kept trying to reconnect. In each case, the Serial Innovator is seeking to understand the entire system well enough to improve it as a whole. They seek a global optimum, rather than a series of local optima. Regardless of the analogy they use to describe their mental processes, they look at ideas and data points they have newly discovered and previously stored away and examine them individually and jointly to discover new connections and relationships.

These four characteristics of curiosity, intuition, creativity, and systems thinking combine to produce an individual who is able to explore situations and create breakthrough ideas during the early stages of identifying and understanding interesting problems. Curiosity is the starting point. As individuals *pursue* their curiosity, they develop expert intuition and become able to combine those characteristics to think systemically. Systems thinking—connecting the dots—requires curiosity and intuition in order to find the right dots, and the development of breakthrough new products requires all three skills in various combinations. This innate combination of skills and abilities is rare and difficult, if not impossible, to develop through training programs.

PERSONALITY CHARACTERISTICS
THAT SUPPORT PROJECT COMPLETION

Creating breakthrough innovation in a large company requires another set of capabilities that enable the Serial Innovator to stay with the project over a long period of time. These personality characteristics include independence, confidence, calculated risk taking, and perseverance.

Independence is a critical characteristic for a Serial Innovator. They are willing to think differently, challenge the organization, and pursue their own ideas to completion. They do not wait for instructions and guidance, electing instead to operate independently. Because their breakthrough projects may last many years, Serial Innovators may have to operate during much of that time as independent agents, making decisions to move forward rather than asking someone else what to do. Several Serial

Innovators observed that other technologists often asked them, "How could you make that decision?" Most employees will stop and ask for permission, but Serial Innovators just move forward, believing that someone will correct them if they get a decision wrong. Although they are happy to explain their decisions if asked, they will undertake tasks that they can complete on their own without seeking approval. Serial Innovators have an independent spirit because they think for themselves, learn by themselves, and "see" the total system.

This independence leads to **confidence**—confidence to act, to decide what to do, and to challenge decisions made by other people. In short, Serial Innovators believe in themselves, in their ideas, and in their projects. The willingness to challenge the organization comes from their confidence. One Serial Innovator described this independent process respectfully, urging all team members to say, "unless otherwise directed" here is what I am going to do. This phrase asserts both independence and confidence in their decision and the direction in which they are going without being overbearing or overly relying on others' decisions.

Breakthrough innovation naturally involves a moderate to high level of risk. Serial Innovators **take calculated risks**, making decisions that are defined as risky by others, but that they see as being reasonable. They perceive these risks as reasonable after conducting in-depth research of their customer, problem, and organization. When they believe customers want and need the product, the organizational risks for developing it are seen as relatively manageable. Their willingness to take risks is directly related to their confidence and convictions about the potential for their ideas and products.

Serial Innovators are not inherently high-risk people. In fact, some of their personal decisions are risk averse. They differ from entrepreneurs because they are unwilling to risk their personal assets to build a business. But when they believe in something, they are willing to risk their jobs at that organization and everything else to pursue that idea.

Finally, **perseverance** is required due to the nature of the development task. In the breakthrough innovation world, there are no quick results. The nature of the task requires a long-term perspective. Serial Innovators are patient, determined, and persevering. Working many years to see results

requires an ability to delay gratification and to look to the future for rewards. Jim Hall, the creator of the Hewlett-Packard (HP) laser-jet printer,
describes his efforts as "eight years to an overnight success" (Lightman
1992). That product required three product embodiment iterations over
eight years, with the first two being commercial failures, before Jim and
his team had learned enough to develop and produce the breakthrough
product.

The combination of personality characteristics required for innovation (independence, confidence, willingness to take calculated risks, and
perseverance) are necessary for Serial Innovators to stay with ideas long
enough to bring the innovations to market. Developing the technologies
and understanding the markets is extremely challenging, and creating organizational movement equally involves patience and persistence. Large
companies and business units within them that have considerable assets
are difficult to move. They focus on current customers and products, and
have momentum pushing them to continue in just that focus. One Serial
Innovator described the organization as a huge block of granite: his job
was to get a drop of mercury under it. And then to just keep pushing on
it, until one day it moved. When the movement happens, there is cause to
celebrate. But movement in these arenas is inevitably gradual, so getting
breakthrough innovations through the organization requires all four of
the characteristics identified above. Those characteristics, plus the ones
required to support creation (curiosity, intuition, creativity, and systems
thinking), are all required for breakthrough innovation and implementation. Either set of characteristics by itself is not sufficient for breakthrough
innovation.

PERSPECTIVES

Serial Innovators have interesting perspectives about business, people, life,
and work. Various authors have called these perspectives one's worldview
or one's values (Hiebert 2008; Naugle 2002). These perspectives develop
predominately from early experiences in life and in the workplace.

Serial Innovators are absolutely clear that the *business must make
money*. If there are no profits, both the company and the customers suffer.
Serial Innovators have observed the realities of business, they know how

business works, and they know what must happen for their companies to be successful. They work to make sure that their products add significant value to their companies. One observed: "The only reason I exist in this company is to make money for the company. If I don't make money for the company, then there's no reason for me to be here."

Another Serial Innovator asked, as we were walking back to his office, "How will this interview increase shareholder value?" He hesitated to talk with us unless we could convince him that it would make a difference to the company. Our answer was to tell him we hoped to help the company learn to understand and manage him more effectively and to identify, develop, and support others like him. As a result, he was willing to spend a couple of hours with us.

Serial Innovators are proud when their products are successful in the marketplace for two reasons: (1) they have made the company more successful and (2) their product ideas mattered to customers, who were willing to spend money to buy them. They frequently knew what impact their products had on the company. One Serial Innovator pulled out a three-by-five card from his desk that had the sales for each product he had developed over his career. This perspective is very different from that of Inventors and basic researchers, who are often content to have technical insights without pushing for customer and market acceptance.

Technology is a means to an end. Inventors tend to see creating new technology as a worthwhile end by itself. Serial Innovators, like Inventors, are supremely technically competent. However, Serial Innovators are focused on customers and see technology as a means to satisfy customer needs. Having customers want and buy their products is their ultimate indicator of success. Technology frequently is necessary to accomplish that success, but Serial Innovators do not tend to get overly focused on the technology. In fact, as we saw in Chapter 2, they only invent when they really have to, preferring to repurpose old technology and borrow solutions from other domains whenever possible. And while Serial Innovators frequently will patent their ideas, they patent only the ideas that they believe can make the company money, not every "cool new idea." They talk about resisting the temptation to just work on cool new ideas. Instead, they focus on what it will take to make a commercial success in the marketplace. Thinking always of the customer, they use technology to solve real problems.

Given their desire to serve customers, Serial Innovators typically are invested in *the greater good*. In other words, they attempt to balance the needs of all interested parties simultaneously: customers, company, team members, and other stakeholders. Looking out for the greater good is one of the factors that defines wise people (Sternberg 2007), suggesting that Serial Innovators are wise in how they fit into and contribute to the world. There is an altruistic side to these Serial Innovators. How can people so bright, curious, and creative also be genuinely good and worry about the welfare of others? One direct quote illustrates this perspective clearly:

I'm always trying to serve the greater good. And that's the simplest thing. However, it's a broad greater good and it encompasses short-term and long-term processes, people in business, risk, and everything else. There's a greater good that integrates everything. Somehow that keeps me grounded and going. And maybe it's hard to quantify it, but it certainly exists in whatever fuzzy or nonfuzzy sense. And that lets me cut through all decisions. It just makes life impeccably easy; even though there are lots of inter-balances. But I'm always serving the greater good.

Earlier, we described Serial Innovators as intrinsically motivated to solve customer problems. Thus, they worry about the welfare of the *customers* and want to design truly useful products for them. As they make development progress, they build up an increasingly strong belief that what they are doing is meaningful to customers, that people are going to like and want the product, and that the product will change people's lives for the better. As Tom Osborn said about the product line he worked on: "That's one of the reasons I like this category [feminine hygiene products]. Our products have made, really made . . . big differences in women's lives. I enjoy that." It may not be a cure for cancer, but in some way this product will make people's lives a little better, easier, or more enjoyable.

Focusing on the greater good for the company is related to the Serial Innovator's commitment to profit. These employees seek to sustain businesses that allow them to pursue interesting problems. This commitment to "common good" for their companies often formed early in their careers.

One Serial Innovator described his early experience observing two different managers:

One manager was totally into the technical stuff we did; that's what drove him. The other person always asked me from the day I walked in the front door, "How does that help the company?" And I realized early on, that's what they want. They want things that help them. They don't want things that just look academically interesting or that are intellectually challenging. They want things that are going to help them. And so I took that hook, line, and sinker.

Serial Innovators described how they wrestled to maintain the proper balance between their love of technology and the greater good of the company. It was easy for one Serial Innovator to go do fun and interesting technical things, but he kept saying, "Why not pick something that is fun *and* interesting *and* beneficial to the company?" In addition to balancing the needs of the company and customers, Serial Innovators have interesting perspectives about people. First, they care deeply about other employees. One Serial Innovator observed that he really wanted to provide jobs for people and was proud to declare that there are "thousands of people in the company now who are employed worldwide because of these inventions."

Frequently, Serial Innovators described coming to their organizations because of the quality of the people there. In fact, one Serial Innovator said he only took the interview with the company to practice for another interview at a place at which he really wanted to work. However, he ultimately accepted the position at the "practice" company because he liked the people in that company much more. Serial Innovators invariably said that they stay in their companies in part because of the talented people and the quality of the people they work with.

Perhaps most important, Serial Innovators recognize the talents and skills other people have to offer and value those abilities. Beyond simply using others' talents to accomplish project goals, they truly value the contributions others can make. As we saw in Chapter 4, these positive perspectives about people enable Serial Innovators to get others to join them on difficult, challenging projects.

Serial Innovators also have a distinctive perspective on their work. They have learned that *it is their lot in life to get the hard problems*, and they *take personal responsibility for achieving results*. Somewhere in their lives, Serial Innovators learned that solving tough problems requires hard work. But they believe that if they focus on a problem long enough and with sufficient creativity, they will be able to discover a good solution. They assume that answers can and will be discovered. They are philosophical in their view that it is their "lot in life" to get the hard problems and do the hard work because they are uniquely prepared to solve those problems. Because of the "lot in life" mentality and their belief in their unique abilities, they assume the personal responsibility to solve the problems and then persist until they do.

In summary, Serial Innovators hold strong worldviews about business, technology, people, and their own role in society. They have well-defined beliefs about the role of companies and profits, and about how they personally fit into that capitalist system. Serial Innovators focus on customers and believe that technology is the means to satisfy customer needs; for them, technology is not the end goal. Although they believe that companies exist to make a profit, they simultaneously focus on the greater good for the customer and the community. They observe the people around them and want to be associated with bright, capable people who are "builders" and want to accomplish things. These perspectives are critical for Serial Innovators and, we assert, for anyone else who would like to lead in our organizations or society.

MOTIVATION

Personality is hardwired into people and is fairly immutable. Perspectives also form early in life and early in one's career, and if they change, they change slowly. Intrinsic motivation derives from the combination of these characteristics. However, motivation also may vary day to day, depending on external factors, such as the culture and management of the firm. Although we describe motivation as a separate characteristic, the deeply intrinsic motivation pattern found in Serial Innovators is closely related to both personality and perspective. Intrinsic motivation is critical for successful creative problem-solving tasks like developing breakthrough new products (Amabile 1988; Deci and Ryan 1985; Pink 2009). The variables of autonomy, purpose, and mastery (Pink 2009) certainly were resident in Serial Innovators. Autonomy is the need for variety, challenge, and choice; mastery is most strongly demonstrated in Serial Innovators' desire for profound understanding; and purpose is found in the desire to solve important customer problems and to see the resulting products changing customers' lives. Managers cannot force people to exert the effort necessary to create breakthrough products. That motivation must come from within. Without intrinsic motivation, there is no breakthrough innovation development.

The initial set of variables surrounding motivation has to do with basic needs and expectations. Serial Innovators need *variety* and *challenges*. Routine, predictable work is not a good use of Serial Innovators' talents. The more difficult the problem, the more Serial Innovators rise to the challenge. One said: "I love hard problems, problems that take years to do—I mean it is fascinating for me [because it] is a very hard problem." Serial Innovators said that hard problems "just make my blood get excited." When tough challenges were not present, they were less satisfied with their jobs. They got bored and did not pay attention to the routine tasks. Notably, Serial Innovators have the patience and perseverance required to work on challenging tasks over several years, but have little or no patience for routine tasks.

Serial Innovators want to do something that no one else has done before. Major obstacles provide the motivation to keep looking, learning, and understanding in order to find solutions. The *joy of discovery* provides additional motivation to keep going. Even though Serial Innovators believe that the purpose of business is to make money, they are more driven by discovery, which arises in part from the innate curiosity in their personalities. They want to do something that no one has done before. They want to find that simple, beautiful pattern in nature that makes everything clear and understandable.

Serial Innovators see unknown territories as opportunities to learn, to find the dots and then to connect those dots in interesting and powerful ways. The desire to learn is a prime motivator for engaging with interesting problems and exploring what might be possible. Motivation to learn and curiosity are very closely related—Serial Innovators just want to know. They take on challenges in domains that are unfamiliar to them, because doing so provides a way for them to learn, to understand, and to make significant contributions. Chuck House's investigation into air pollution is a great example of just this. Chuck is an electrical engineer, not an environmental engineer. However, because he was diagnosed with emphysema, he was driven to learn about this new domain. In the end, his drive to understand this phenomenon led to new laws governing polluters.

Tough challenges and the joy of discovery lead to the next motivational characteristic—the *drive for profound understanding*. Serial Innovators have to understand for themselves the problems on which they are working. This level of understanding differs from the level necessary for other professions. In disciplines like management, the standard is the depth of understanding that is required to make an informed decision. In engineering and other scientific disciplines, however, the standard of understanding is the depth required to create. Complete mastery of the problem is required to create a breakthrough new product. And mastery is one of the key elements critical to intrinsic motivation (Pink 2009).

The sought-for level of mastery requires complete dedication to and immersion in the problem. To understand something deeply, Serial Innovators have to live it and develop their own sense about what is important through firsthand experiences. Fundamentally, they live, eat, drink, and sleep the problem until it becomes their lives. When Serial Innovators select an important problem, they become thoroughly immersed in it. They dive deeply into the problem, relish in understanding all aspects of it, and master its individual elements at the level required to synthesize and create something that never before existed.

Serial Innovators are not simply satisfied to understand the problems they have chosen to address; they have to use that understanding to produce a useful result that will impact the company and society. Serial Innovators want to impact their companies and communities in the best possible ways. Just as they want to solve *tough* problems, they also need to make the *optimal* impact. They are not content with a good solution to the problem; they want to find the "one best solution" and then prove that it works. Serial Innovators stay with their projects much longer than most people in new product development (NPD) because they need to see their product in the hands of customers. They are motivated by the tangible "Gee, I made this happen" feeling. When a project reaches a point of proving the product in the manufacturing plant and the rest of the team is being reassigned, Serial Innovators are often adamant about sticking with the project through commercialization. One said, "I really want to finish. I don't want to turn the project over to somebody else . . . I want to finish it." Remaining on the project through the execution phase allows them to see what they planned and created come to fruition. Seeing the products being made and sold is a validation of their ideas, passion, creativity, and innovation results. This aspect of motivation obviously derives from and renews Serial Innovators' perseverance, as well as their desire to create for a greater good.

Serial Innovators are intrinsically motivated to solve customer problems. They need variety and challenges. The joy of discovery and of understanding profoundly fuel their enduring motivation. Serial Innovators also are results-oriented; they want to see the products in the hands of customers and for those customers to be delighted. It is clear that these motivations arise from, link to, and reinforce numerous aspects of their personalities and worldviews. However, we discuss them separately from those other characteristics of Serial Innovators because day-to-day mismanagement of them can very quickly lead to job dissatisfaction and even to them leaving an organization to look for a situation that would more adequately facilitate their breakthrough innovation process. As depicted in Figure 5.1, it is the combination of personality, perspective, and motivation that drives Serial Innovators to pursue the knowledge needed technically to create and to manage the process and the politics of development in the organization. The next section explicates how they prepare to innovate.

PREPARATION

Serial Innovators' preparation for success differs significantly from that of other technologists. Inventors typically prepare deeply in one technology domain, most frequently through formal education and even advanced degrees. Implementers also use formal education to prepare technically; however, their education focuses on applied technology problems rather than learning how to conduct research. They also may obtain additional training (formally or informally on the job) in project management. Serial Innovators, however, need to learn significantly across multiple domains: business, customer, and political, in addition to the technology domain. Kelley and Littman (2000) coined the term "T-shaped people" to refer to individuals who have this type of broad industry, customer, and business knowledge, but who also have deep technical knowledge. Serial Innovators develop just the sort of breadth found in T-shaped people. However, they also develop deep technical knowledge across multiple technical areas. They thus may be better described as being "dynamic Ts" or even "π-shaped people" (Macaulay et al. 2010; Miles and Jones 2008): individuals with a breadth of learning across domains, but with great depth of learning in multiple technical domains.

We explicitly asked the Serial Innovators we interviewed how they prepared for and learned about the various topics that were necessary to breakthrough innovate successfully. We analyzed their responses in two ways that are framed in Table 5.1. First, we identified several content areas that required preparation:

1. Basic technical skills;

2. Deep knowledge across multiple technical domains;

3. Business understanding;

4. Customer understanding;

5. Process knowledge; and

6. Political skills.

Then we examined the mechanisms they used to accomplish their preparation:

1. Formal education;

2. Guided or mentored by others;

3. On-the-job observation; and

4. Self-study.

Across our Serial Innovator interviews, 142 total mentions were made of how they obtained the different types learning they needed.

TABLE 5.1 Preparation content and mechanisms

	Technical	Multiple domains	Business	Customers	Process	Politics	Total/ percent
Formal education	6/ 18.7%	2/ 6.1%	4/ 25.0%	0	3/ 11.1%	0	15/ 10.6%
Guide or mentor	3/ 9.4%	0	3/ 18.7%	1/ 6.2%	5/ 18.5%	3/ 16.6%	15/ 10.6%
On-the-job	12/ 37.5%	8/ 24.2%	6/ 37.6%	8/ 50.0%	12/ 44.5%	10/ 55.6%	56/ 39.4%
Self-study	11/ 34.3%	23/ 69.7%	3/ 18.7%	7/ 43.8%	7/ 25.9%	5/ 27.8%	56/ 39.4%
Total/percent	32/ 22.5%	33/ 23.3%	16/ 11.3%	16/ 11.3%	27/ 19.0%	18/ 12.6%	142/ 100%

Some interesting patterns emerge from Table 5.1. First, on-the-job learning and self-study dominate the modes of preparation, constituting almost 80% of the content learning across all topics. Formal education may have provided Serial Innovators initial knowledge about their primary technical domains. However, it did not (and perhaps could not) give them the knowledge they need to become T- or π-shaped people. Almost 70% of the preparation for understanding across multiple technical domains occurs through self-study. It takes considerable personal effort to learn about new technologies and interdisciplinary problems and opportunities. A little of that preparation may take place through typical on-the-job tasks and experiences, but most of it is intrinsically motivated and done through self-study—usually outside the normal workday.

Serial Innovators are powerful observers and learners. If they need or want to know something, they go learn it, relying on their observation skills and on their abilities and willingness to learn for themselves. The breadth and depth of their curiosity drives interests in many topics and issues, and they dive deeply into them to understand completely. As systems thinkers, they need to understand the entire system on which they focus—whether that is a technical system or an organizational one. They drive for profound understanding and derive great joy from the discovery of new knowledge, insights, and products. And they want to accomplish significant results that are good for the customer, the company, and their colleagues. All of these factors make Serial Innovators incredible learners, who are not afraid to tackle any problem. And they do this over and over again.

The methods used for learning and preparation across different topics vary considerably. When preparing to address business issues, Serial Innovators use a bit of each of the learning methods to gain the needed knowledge. They take a flexible approach to learning about business issues, and they do not use formal education methods to learn about customers or politics. Serial Innovators learn about customers from on-the-job experiences and from self-study, whereas on-the-job preparation is the primary way in which Serial Innovators learn about politics. These trends imply that observation, trial and error, and reflection on positive and negative practices are more important for learning about these topics than formal training, management guidance, or mentoring.

For those concerned about supporting and developing Serial Innovators, there are some important implications from the data in Table 5.1. First, there may be a large opportunity for our formal education systems to help prepare technology graduates to deal with customers and with the political realities of organizations. Furthermore, there may be opportunities for organizations to do more with managers and mentors to engage with and coach potential Serial Innovators, especially for learning in these domains. However, the most important item to recognize is the role of personal drive and intrinsic motivation in the preparation of potential Serial Innovators.

SUMMARY
Understanding the above characteristics will help to identify and develop potential Serial Innovators, as will be discussed in more depth in Chapter 6. These characteristics also are useful to help elucidate the complex interactions across personality factors, perspectives, motivation, and preparation that enable Serial Innovators to tackle seemingly impossible problems, to find and understand customer problems, to struggle to achieve organizational acceptance, and to stay with problems for several years until results are achieved and customers have the products in their hands. Table 5.2

TABLE 5.2 Integrating process and characteristics

	Personality	Motivation	Perspective	Preparation
Find and understand	Curiosity Systems thinking Creativity Intuitive	Variety Challenge Profound understanding	Business and profit Greater good • Customer • Company	Learning agility
Invent and validate	Systems thinking Creativity Curiosity Perseverance Independence Risk taking	Joy of discovery Results	Technology is a means to an end Greater good • Team Tough problems are my lot in life	Learning agility
Execute and create market acceptance	Perseverance Risk taking	Results	Greater good • Customer	Learning agility

shows the relationships between the characteristics described here and the processes outlined in Chapter 2.

Finding and understanding interesting and important problems requires the personality characteristics of curiosity, intuition, creativity, and systems thinking—along with the motivation to seek challenges and to understand profoundly. When those characteristics are melded with perspectives about business and serving the greater good, as well as thorough preparation and agile learning, Serial Innovators have the potential to solve problems that are profoundly important to customers and to the world.

As Serial Innovators move toward inventing and validating, they rely on the characteristics described above on top of their inherent proclivities for independence, perseverance, and risk taking. They are confident in their proposals and are starting to sense the joys of discovery that are necessary to sustain themselves through these project stages. At this stage, the Serial Innovator demonstrates the tenacity and persistence required to solve tough problems. Previous preparation plus ongoing, flexible learning continue to play a key role for the Serial Innovator.

These same characteristics continue to be important as Serial Innovators execute projects and create market acceptance. Although Serial Innovators continue in a leadership and ambassadorial role during these phases, their hands-on developmental role usually diminishes as more people become involved to make the product a reality, produce it, and market and distribute it to customers. But the Serial Innovator remains engaged and pushes to see the product used by the customer, while continuing to learn what other problems need to be solved in future projects. These personality characteristics, perspectives, motivations, and preparation techniques—and the interactions among them—uniquely qualify Serial Innovators to find, understand, and solve important problems, as well as to create breakthrough products and bring them to market.

6 IDENTIFYING AND DEVELOPING SERIAL INNOVATORS

Many Serial Innovators have voiced concerns that their companies would not have hired them today if they were just coming into the workforce, despite their unique set of characteristics that we described in Chapter 5. For example, Serial Innovators describe themselves as having a "predisposition to expect connections." They see things that others do not see, dive deeper than others dive, understand more profoundly, and challenge the status quo more directly. Although they are by no means wild-eyed misfits, they differ from the employees that human resource managers have developed interview templates to find.

This chapter provides insight and advice on three key issues to help your firm:

1. Identify the potential Serial Innovators in your company today.

2. Nurture potential Serial Innovators into full-fledged Serial Innovators who create significant new products for the firm.

3. Work around your company's systems that may tend to screen out hiring and developing potential Serial Innovators.

IDENTIFYING POTENTIAL SERIAL INNOVATORS
To identify Serial Innovators early, determine whether one can discern the differences—other than their explicit record of financial success—between

proven Serial Innovators and others of comparable age and years in an industry whose contributions fall just short of this standard of excellence. There are, in fact, clear differences between those who are exceptional Serial Innovators and those who are lower-impact product developers, Inventors, or Champions. With only rare exceptions, the distinction is unmistakable.

Identifying potential breakthrough Serial Innovators cannot be accomplished merely by employing a mechanistic, objective checklist. On the other hand, it need not and should not be left entirely to chance. Identification, instead, combines a search for some specific and necessary (but not sufficient) personal characteristics with other, more subjective capabilities that can only be seen through developing an engaged relationship with the potential Serial Innovator of the type described in the next chapter. As one manager put it, before you really get to know them, it is difficult to separate out the potential Serial Innovators from the "wild ducks." Thus, he found that he had to support all of the wild ducks in his organization as if they were Serial Innovators, until he could discern who had the capability to create breakthrough innovations and who was just going to keep throwing out new ideas that either had no market or could not be developed. Identifying potential Serial Innovators is a skilled form of discovery, just like the process of breakthrough innovation itself. Because identifying potential Serial Innovators is not a strictly formulaic process, it is critical for managers to invest in developing their own skills for doing so.

Identifying true potential Serial Innovators requires looking at the mix of how several important differentiating characteristics manifest themselves *collectively* in the individual. The five identifiable characteristics that all potential Serial Innovators have are as follows:

1. Systems thinking: the ability to connect the dots across seemingly disparate pieces of information, perhaps from different knowledge domains;

2. Above-average levels of creativity (but not extreme levels);

3. Innate curiosity that extends across multiple knowledge domains;

4. The ability to develop intuition based on deep expertise; and

5. The intrinsic motivation to make things "better."

Of all the explicitly differentiating characteristics found in Serial Innovators, these are the early indicators, as they are skills that are innate (they likely cannot be developed) and as all five must be resident. When looking for potential Serial Innovators in the initial hiring process, screening for these characteristics is crucial. Yet although these are necessary characteristics, they are not sufficient for identifying individuals with a strong propensity to become Serial Innovators.

Crucially, these characteristics manifest themselves collectively in the individual. Looking for the whole differentiates the real potential Serial Innovator from those who display these characteristics without the ability to integrate them all effectively. At each career stage, there will be indicators of how Serial Innovators or potential Serial Innovators engage differently with:

- Understanding problems;
- Undertaking projects;
- Considering business solutions; and
- Connecting with people.

These capabilities appear in the order in which Serial Innovators tend to cultivate them. Even very early in their careers, potential Serial Innovators engage differently with problems than other people, but they usually develop business acumen and people skills later—and this is something that managers who identify them early based on their personal and problem-solving characteristics can help jump-start.

The first category, understanding problems, is significantly rarer than the others and can be screened for within the first year of work at the firm. Project engagement skills can be determined shortly thereafter, because Serial Innovators must demonstrate the ability to persist over the long term. Innovating requires hard work and long-term perseverance. Then, Serial Innovators must be willing to learn about strategy and the business to understand technology as a means to make profit. Finally, the fourth capability provides the perspective and wisdom necessary to have a breakthrough product accepted by the organization and brought to market.

Within the first category—*how they engage with problems*—curiosity is an important indicator. If someone is not highly curious, it is best simply to move to the next candidate. Curiosity consists of having multiple interests and exploring those interests very deeply. Although perhaps not the most important personal characteristic, it is easier to screen for than some of the others. Curiosity helps drive both creativity and systems thinking. Without curiosity, it is unlikely that someone can be constructively creative or explore sufficiently deeply to "connect the dots" of powerful systems thinking. Creativity can be determined through standardized tests and scales. Even though Serial Innovators are more creative than the average person in the population, they are not two or three standard deviations more creative. Extreme creativity is not necessary.

"Connecting the dots," taking disparate pieces of information from different domains and making links among these data points to understand problems in new ways, is the most important aspect of problem engagement—and the most difficult to discern just from a short interaction with an individual, such as one has in an interview situation. Uncovering this capability will take some creative questioning and perhaps more of an engaged relationship.

Intrinsic motivation drives curious individuals to expand the breadth of their interests and the rigor and depth of their analysis; it is necessary for solving tough problems, profoundly understanding, and pursuing results. Finally, their ability to trust their own intuition across all of these topics adds a level of sophistication and capability to the other characteristics. The result is a person who goes beyond investigating an assigned problem, and who seeks to understand the problem in multiple contexts and from multiple perspectives.

Within the second category—*how they engage with projects*—persistence, hard work, and personal responsibility characteristics are the easiest to identify, because they complement and bring to life Serial Innovators' problem engagement capabilities. Without persistence, hard work, and feeling a personal responsibility for the project's success, it is unlikely that someone will bring breakthrough innovations to market.

Potential breakthrough Serial Innovators are distinguished by a combination of confidence and independence, which enables them to support taking calculated risks—especially in the paths they take to solve technical problems. However, the project engagement capabilities of independence, confidence, and risk taking can be misused without the presence of the other three types of engagement capabilities (persistence, hard work, and personal responsibility). Without these engagement capabilities, overconfidence and independence could result in taking risks that are unlikely to lead to profitable new breakthrough products.

Interestingly, the personal drive associated with project engagement capabilities is common to both Serial Innovators and Inventors (those inclined toward insight and technical discovery, but not motivated to move a product to market); these capabilities will not differentiate between them. However, the *magnitude* of these capabilities will differentiate those Serial Innovators and Inventors with the potential to be top performers from those who are more average.

It is the third category of capabilities—*how they engage with the business*—that significantly differentiates Serial Innovators from other development personnel, especially Inventors. They come to perceive business in the following terms:

- Business must make money.
- Technology is a means to an end.
- Pursuing the greater good for both the company and customers is the right thing to do.

Although Serial Innovators may not graduate from school with this orientation in place, they will start to develop these attitudes very early in their careers. Note that this engagement orientation is critical to keeping them from becoming pure technologists who are technically very capable, but who pursue technology for technology's sake without a clear focus on customer outcomes.

Finally, *how they engage with people* differentiates Serial Innovators from other development employees, including people who have the potential to become high-impact Inventors. Successful Serial Innovators sincerely value others and recognize that their contributions are absolutely necessary for effective innovation. They also use positive influence techniques to achieve goals, rather than using power or personal authority to do so.

Although they may be naturally inclined to value the unique capabilities of other people, many of their specific techniques for engaging with people professionally develop during the early part of their careers.

The Appendix provides questions and discussion scenarios that will help identify potential Serial Innovators. These questions are organized to help managers discern whether the five critical characteristics are likely present, and are then followed by groups of questions and discussion scenarios to help managers ascertain employee capabilities in each of the four engagement arenas: problems, projects, business, and people. Some of these can be used in initial intervals (short interactions) and hiring situations; others will be more helpful in longer-term interactions that occur later in a potential Serial Innovator's career.

Crucially, this outline and the questions and discussion scenarios of the Appendix are not the complete answer to identifying potential Serial Innovators. Identifying Serial Innovators is like becoming a wine connoisseur—both forms of expertise require an integrative and enduring attention to detail. The skill of identifying potential Serial Innovators is based on understanding the whole person and on recognizing a complex pattern of interacting characteristics and capabilities. A Serial Innovator is not merely the sum of their characteristics. Discernment of subtleties and synergies is necessary to identify potential Serial Innovators. It takes practice. The challenge is to use the characteristics and engagement capabilities defined above as a starting point to learn how to identify potential breakthrough Serial Innovators. Take the time to reflect on the practice and understanding required to identify potential Serial Innovators.

NURTURING POTENTIAL SERIAL INNOVATORS

Using the questions in the Appendix, you believe you have hired a technologist who has the potential to become a Serial Innovator. Now you need to both give him the opportunity to use the capabilities he already possesses to contribute to the firm's technology development needs and help him develop the additional capabilities he will need to grow into a breakthrough Serial Innovator.

Remember that Serial Innovators are rather rare. Thus, not all of those whom you hire as potential Serial Innovators actually will be able to develop into one. The purpose of the next section is to recommend ways for you to sort those who have the ability to become Serial Innovators from those who are a better fit in another role. However, remember that just because someone is unlikely to become a Serial Innovator does not mean that the individual will not become a valued technical employee. He or she may well develop into a strong Inventor, Implementer, or even manager of technologists. The goal is to determine early what path is best for what individual.

Zero to Five Years in Industry

The first few years of a technologist's career are essential for establishing many of the skills and work patterns that will determine their ability to become a Serial Innovator. Potential Serial Innovators first need to prove their technical capabilities by solving meaningful problems. It is the time to perform exceptionally against the expectations of the organization, develop a technical track record, and make significant technical contributions. You are looking for performance like that exhibited by Dave in understanding the nut roasting process. Only if their performance is seen as exceptional will they be likely to gain credibility as significant contributors, which will in turn give them the time to develop the other capabilities demonstrated by Serial Innovators.

During these years, managers need to be aware of the job assignments given to those who are thought to have the potential to become Serial Innovators. Successfully completed, complex job assignments are key to predicting successful performance five years in the future (Thompson et al. 1974). Young technologists usually are not given the latitude to find their own assignments, so managers need to actively manage the technical problems potential Serial Innovators (at this point, all of the "wild ducks") are assigned, to ensure that they are challenging and complex. Challenging job assignments will contain difficult technical problems, but they also may contain other complications such as time constraints or requirements to work with groups or departments in other disciplines. For these assigned tasks, expect potential Serial Innovators to demonstrate more curiosity and more initiative around expanding the assignment beyond the explicitly given task.

Early in their careers, technologists can gain excellent exposure to customers. It is important that they visit customers, see products and services in use in context, and begin to understand the subtleties and nuances associated with different customers and customer groups. It also is important for them to learn how to talk to customers and to ask the appropriate, probing questions that will reveal insights about how consumers interact with products and services. Potential Serial Innovators should also be exposed to the competitors' technologies so that they can learn to balance customer input against existing technological possibilities. Should your skilled technologist show no inclination to continue to interact with customers after they have been introduced to several and learned how to talk to them, he or she likely will develop into an Inventor, Implementer, or technical manager rather than a Serial Innovator.

Many of the perspectives described in Chapter 5 are shaped and reinforced early in a Serial Innovator's career. The view that technology is a means to an end can be reinforced or extinguished, depending on early experiences; a manager who mentors about the value (to the customer, financially to the firm, or for the general good) of solving a particular problem will help reinforce that perspective. Additionally, exposure to customers with real pain points can reinforce their intrinsic motivation to contribute to the greater good with technical solutions.

Finally, potential Serial Innovators need to begin to learn about organizational politics and the necessity of selling their ideas within the company. By the end of this stage of their careers, they must have "crossed the bridge" from political naïveté to political pragmatist (see Chapter 4). Ideally, they would learn about these issues by watching other senior technologists wrestle with selling their ideas and projects into the commercialization process. Unfortunately, most research and development (R&D) personnel do not see idea selling as part of their job descriptions, and thus most potential Serial Innovators are not likely to be able to learn from their senior colleagues. In those cases, managers intent on developing their capabilities can expose them to other, well-known project Champions in the organization for mentoring.

Additional mechanisms for supporting potential Serial Innovators' further development include the following:

1. Work trade show booths, especially at trade shows where new products are introduced. They need to work the booth, talk to potential customers, and walk the floor, investigating what competitors are doing.

2. Accompany service technicians, especially to customers who have had a catastrophic failure.

3. Work with a mentor from marketing or strategy who exposes them to the strategies and marketing capabilities of the firm.

4. Take classes in new product development (NPD) and commercialization, business strategy, market research, and marketing. Negotiation and interpersonal behavior may also be helpful.*

Although most Serial Innovators do not emerge for at least five years, those initial five years are critical for confirming their excellence in technical performance (problem and project engagement), developing their business and people engagement capabilities, and reinforcing their perspectives about the financial and humanitarian value of solving important customer problems.

Five to Ten Years in Industry
Most Serial Innovators begin to emerge as uniquely skilled contributors after working within a firm for over five years. Having learned the basics about the industry technology base and intrafirm politics, these individuals now begin to differentiate themselves. By this point in their careers, they have established reputations as curious, engaged systems thinkers. Their intrinsic motivation to solve difficult problems has become apparent. They have persevered on more than one project, perhaps driving a product to market or engendering the trust and respect of their peers and senior management.

This is a critical turning point in their careers for effective, efficient personal development. At this level, you are investing in high-potential,

---

* Most companies have requirements for one to two weeks a year of ongoing training and education, handled between a combination of internally and externally offered short courses. Potential Serial Innovators could maximize the benefits of this company-wide requirement by taking classes that cultivate their innate skills.

high-performing individuals. As such, personal apprenticeship—not necessarily coaching or mere mentoring—with experienced, successful Serial Innovators and managers can be justified. Apprenticeship is not simply telling them what to do; instead it involves getting them engaged in the practice of innovation alongside those in your organization who already are truly expert at it (assuming that there are some in your organization).

Those guiding these rare individuals should find multiple ways to get them engaged with customers. Further, they should challenge the nascent Serial Innovator to identify interesting and important problems to address. Finally, they should provide opportunities to witness firsthand interactions with all levels of senior management across multiple functions throughout the firm.

Managers should not facilitate all of the Serial Innovators' growth—it is of critical importance that these individuals begin self-directed learning. Interestingly, at a point in their careers where many technical personnel seek, or already have completed, MBAs, very few Serial Innovators take this route to increase their business knowledge. They predominantly obtain their knowledge of business "on the job" and from their managers. The most successful Serial Innovators are great observers and self-directed learners. As such, they predominantly eschew more formal education after completing their technical degrees; instead, by following their almost instinctive curiosity, they dig deeply on their own as they seek new insights that could lead to breakthrough innovations. An ideal example of such informal, personal engagement occurred when one Serial Innovator needed to gain insight in microbiology:

I go find the simplest book I can find. Sometimes it is a high school text or a first-year college text, and I read that. Now it doesn't mean that I have to be . . . an expert in microbiology. But I have to know a lot, enough, to really understand and delve deeply. Can I go in and do microbiological techniques and some of those sophisticated techniques microbiologists use today? No, I can't. I don't even attempt to. But I can hold my own in some of the discussions with company microbiologists, or any consultant outside the company that we bring in. I cannot be an expert. But I can take a few areas and mine them relatively deeply.

Separating True Serial Innovators from Those Who Have Only Some of the Capabilities

A number of the senior technical staff may exhibit several characteristics of Serial Innovators, yet may be unsuited for further development in this line if they do not exhibit comprehensive systems thinking, select only the most commercially promising problems on which to work, or demonstrate a deep underlying motivation. Those whose interest is limited to the self-gratifying or pure technology problem should not be expected to emerge as successful Serial Innovators. Additionally, some aspects of an individual's nature can become so fixed at this stage of life that important change is virtually impossible. In particular, if an individual has not "crossed the bridge" to understand the necessary role that managing the politics of the firm plays in serving customer needs, they may already have settled into serving the firm as an Inventor, rather than a Serial Innovator.

On the other hand, those who have the personal characteristics of Serial Innovators, those who exhibit strong behavior or potential in three of the four categories of engagement capabilities, and those who exhibit strong determination to contribute as Serial Innovators may still require opportunities to begin engaging with the firm politically. For example, one mid-career potential Serial Innovator met all the major criteria, but was frustrated because he could not get the acceptance of the organization; he had not crossed the political bridge. In his case, it was from ignorance of the necessity to do so, rather than from a lack of willingness. After reading about our research findings on the importance of managing the politics of innovation, he realized that he had not fully engaged the problem of gaining organizational acceptance. Once he focused on that problem, and applied his creativity and systems thinking to the organizational side of the problem, he became incredibly successful. Sometimes, he lamented having to learn about and work on those political issues, but he became very good, very quickly.

Even if a technologist exhibits most of the positive behaviors, one must ask whether he or she is doing so at the level to be expected of the most senior contributors in the firm. Are these people working on great, or merely good, problems? Do they have a track record of engaging the organization in such a way that moves it to meaningful change? Have they demonstrated the perseverance and calculated risk taking necessary to bring something new and big to the market? Such an assessment will indicate who has the capability to contribute at higher levels, and it will provide insight about how best to foster each employee's growth.

Several options can be employed for supporting technologists who exhibit great potential in engaging problems, projects, businesses, and people. If they are good in all four sets of engagement capabilities, merely giving them the freedom—the time and resources necessary—to find interesting problems and pursue them may be all the development that is needed. Further, by betting that they have the capability and potential to become Serial Innovators, you signal a level of confidence that they will aspire to meet. Connecting them with others with such potential is another means of development. Their mutual sharing of experience, particularly in areas of common challenge (such as navigating the organization), offers the opportunity for developing the organization's culture, as well as the individual's potential.

Those with Proven Capability

Late-career technologists (fifteen-plus years) either have the skill to innovate on a grand scale or they don't. Little benefit is expected from attempting to foster those who have not already succeeded as Serial Innovators. However, Serial Innovators who already have been successful can continue to grow if they are deployed as productively as possible. If they are aligned with the most important problems and innovation issues in the firm, and assigned the most insightful, relational managers to work with (see Chapter 7), they will continue to produce important innovations. Assign these important problems on the basis of proven skill and organizational needs.

Many Serial Innovators continue to persevere and seek tough challenges throughout long careers. One Serial Innovator related how, in his early sixties, he put himself on a committee that had nothing to do with technology or innovation in order to learn how to work with a group of people with whom he had never worked but who could be important to a future project. Serial Innovators' strong intrinsic motivation to solve important problems continues to push them to do extraordinary things at a point in their lives when others are seeking a smoother, easier road.

Nonetheless, breakthrough innovation projects take considerable time and energy. An organization and key managers need to use the talent that exists wisely, and to discern whether a more mature Serial Innovator still has the energy required to fight a long, hard battle to innovate and commercialize the next breakthrough product. Frank discussions are always key when dealing with such issues. Serial Innovators can also be used to identify and develop the next generation of Serial Innovators. Those with proven capability are most likely, of all employees in the firm, to have the insight to see how current policy and practice will impact the career development pipeline of future Serial Innovators.

EXPLICITLY MANAGING THE SERIAL INNOVATOR PIPELINE
We have observed four different "systems" for identifying and developing Serial Innovators, as illustrated in Table 6.1.

Companies in the "Losing the Formula" category have had and perhaps still have some proven Serial Innovators—as well as a few other individuals who have demonstrated most of the capabilities—but have no corporate emphasis on identifying and developing these capabilities early in technologists' careers. Frequently, these are the companies that enabled these "different" people to survive a decade or two ago, but have shifted their emphasis to incremental improvements. By treating employees homogeneously, these companies can hinder innovative talent early in technologists' careers. Without any way to prove themselves in more innovative projects, potential Serial Innovators leave this type of firm for greener pastures.

TABLE 6.1   Firm pipelines of innovator identification and development

Firm situation	Innovator presence New hires	0–5 years	5–10 years	Near innovators	Proven innovators
Losing the formula	—	—	—	☺	☺
One-hit wonders	—	—	☺	—	—
Talent rich and innovator light	☺	☺	☺	—	—
Fruitful system	☺	☺	☺	☺	☺

A number of firms have one or more individuals who have been successful in creating and introducing a "One-Hit Wonder" that was either a breakthrough product or a significant category enhancement. But to date, they have produced only one such innovation. The question becomes: will they ever be able to do it again and become true Serial Innovators? In these cases, the initial effort of bringing the first project to market took a huge personal toll on the Innovator—personally and politically—because of the culture of the organization. Organizational cultures that make it difficult to develop something novel discourage serial innovation. If there is no recognition of the importance of these types of contributions from others in the organization (especially senior managers), the probability of a proven Innovator developing future breakthrough products declines. Intrinsic motivation is difficult to sustain in strongly resistant environments.

In the "Talent Rich and Innovator Light" firm, organizational leaders believe that there are highly capable technologists in the organization—and by any objective measure there are. However, that highly capable talent rarely produces a commercially successful breakthrough new product. Although the organizational leaders espouse innovation and exhort employees to develop new products, the culture and the systems rarely produce the desired result. This pattern is almost always a leadership and management problem, where the organizational systems reward and encourage behavior that is not consistent with breakthrough innovation. As described in Chapters 1 and 2, there are a host of reasons these organizations focus on optimizing and improving what exists and are reluctant to invest the dollars and (more important) the time to stay with promising projects and potential Serial Innovators long enough to see the breakthrough results. The result is that, while Inventors abound, potential Serial Innovators again leave for greener pastures, and the firm frequently is unable to commercialize products from new technologies developed in their labs.

Even when a firm operates a "Fruitful System" for identifying and supporting Serial Innovators across their careers, organizational leaders worry about their ability to sustain these efforts and work diligently to consciously enhance their Serial Innovator support systems. The Serial Innovators in those firms also actively work to improve support mechanisms and to resist the organizational pressures that tend to focus on incremental improvements, driving Serial Innovators and breakthrough innovations out.

Identifying, developing, and supporting Serial Innovators is difficult because they differ from the "average" technologist and because they need individualized management (see Chapter 7). It takes both corporate systems and the sensitized capabilities of individual managers to put in place a fruitful system that enables them to contribute to the firm in a steady stream. Sometimes, it is the corporate hiring practices of a firm that contribute significantly to a firm's inability to bring potential Serial Innovators into the firm.

INHERENT CHALLENGES IN CONTEMPORARY CORPORATE HIRING PRACTICES—AND HOW TO OVERCOME THEM

As noted at the outset of this chapter, a number of Serial Innovators across several firms believe they would be screened out of their company's current hiring practices. In large corporations, college recruitment of new technical staff often is delegated to a relatively small number of non-innovation-savvy staff (most often, human resources staff). These recruiters represent multiple business units and corporate groups to achieve recruiting economies of scale and scope. Such individuals are highly qualified to assess critical interpersonal aptitudes; however, they lack the expertise to discern many of the requisite skills for breakthrough innovation, such as systems thinking. As a result, initial interview and hiring decisions often are based on more measurable, quantifiable criteria, such as grade point average and demonstrated university leadership (even for technologists).

In actuality, these hiring practices may hinder the identification of future potential Serial Innovators. These practices assume that the skills required for breakthrough innovation are a subset of, or subsidiary to, technical and leadership skills, and concomitantly that Serial Innovators will naturally emerge from this larger pool of standardly recruited talent. But this recruiting process squeezes out variation. A mechanistic approach to hiring, while yielding highly reproducible results, in fact reduces the numbers of high-potential candidates who might have made their way through the identification process if the recruiting profile were focused on the ability to innovate.

Whereas technical recruiting has been made into a relatively explicit, recipe-driven, high-volume process, a more nuanced, individual process of discerning and discovering talent is required to locate potential future Serial Innovators. Serial Innovators are characterized in terms of both their "know-what" (their deep and broad interests and specializations) and their "know-how" (their thirst for discovery and conceptual learning, rather than rote memorization). Whereas grade point averages measure mastery of candidates' "know-what" about the theory in technical domains, practical applications awareness is not assessed by grades. More important, grade point averages do not reveal an individual's aptitude for discovery ("know-how"), a critical feature of a Serial Innovator's creativity.

Separately, students who establish a track record of leadership can broadly be categorized into two distinct groups. The first group seeks leadership as a natural result of their desire to serve others, most often their fellow students. However, the second group, of significant size, does so in an attempt merely to develop the record itself. These students are not motivated by solving others' problems; as such, they represent the antithesis of the most successful corporate Serial Innovators.

Mass recruiting policies also unintentionally sacrifice personal connections. Many Serial Innovators discussed the importance of people—especially managers, coworkers, and senior executives—in their decision to accept a position, in their job satisfaction, and in considering leaving a position. By only minimally involving such attractors in the recruiting process, advantage could easily go to competitors who have technical personnel involved in recruiting. Furthermore, having innovation-savvy people recruiting new technical talent significantly increases the probability that the more tacit capabilities that differentiate potential Serial Innovators from Inventors and others will be recognized. Eliminating personnel from the early stages of the screening and hiring process who implicitly understand how potential Serial Innovators "look" will likely delimit breakthrough innovation expertise from coming into the pipeline.

Based on the preceding observations, we recommend a much more individualized and specific recruiting process for potential Serial Innovators. First, we recommend engaging Serial Innovators and Serial Innovator managers in the recruiting. They will be more attuned to Serial Innovator skills, capabilities, and tendencies than will others who have been prepared to screen primarily on GPA and leadership skills. Second, we recommend a much more engaged process for recruiting. Rather than posting positions and passively seeing who applies, it will be necessary to proactively use the firm's technologists' network, actively engaging innovative faculty connections across multiple universities to help look for and recruit potential Serial Innovators. Third, the types of questions and conversations in initial interviews need to be quite different from the standard human resources process. Specific suggestions for questions to be used in that interview are included in the Appendix. Many of the desired characteristics will not be fully formed in undergraduate or even graduate students, but the disposition and tendencies will be there. Asking questions such as those in the Appendix can help experts sift through candidates in the initial screening process.

SUMMARY

Large international corporations spend millions identifying and developing managers to optimize Serial Innovators' potential. Yet relatively little is spent identifying and developing nascent Serial Innovators to generate the future growth that companies need. This chapter has described a process for assessing the presence of Serial Innovators within a company and has outlined methods for identifying and developing Serial Innovators at various stages in their careers. The key factors for identification are to assess how Serial Innovators engage with: (1) problems, (2) projects, (3) business, and (4) people. Finally, we identify limitations associated with current recruitment practices and recommend a richer and more robust recruitment process to find the unique talent associated with Serial Innovators.

7   MANAGING SERIAL
INNOVATORS FOR IMPACT

By now, we expect that you are thinking, "We have people like this. It's just that we didn't know they existed elsewhere." So, having identified these rare, but not uncommon, employees, and having gained insight into who they are and how they work, what are the best practices for managing these unique, exceptional individuals? As one Serial Innovator suggested, we advise you to "let the birds fly!" But what does this really mean, and how will you implement it? This chapter provides guidance as to how to best manage Serial Innovators.

MANAGING PERSONNEL IN LARGE, MATURE FIRMS

To gain perspective on managing Serial Innovators, it is important to begin by reviewing the basis for most management practices in large, mature firms. These firms seek significant financial return and growth at minimum risk. To accomplish these objectives, large firms—and the processes used to manage within them—are designed to deliver certain competitive advantages, including economies of scale and scope and embedded organizational knowledge. As a result, as companies grow, management policy and practice typically become increasingly mechanistic.

Start-ups and small firms hire friends of the initial founding team and colleagues from previous firms. People pitch in and do whatever is required to sustain the firm. Job titles are rather haphazard, the hierarchy below the CEO and president may be a bit muddled, and there are no clear "career paths." Management policies, including hiring, evaluation, promotion, and recognition of employees, become increasingly formal, structured, and standardized as firms mature. The firm moves from ad hoc management practices to "professional management." Structure and standardization underlie efficient systems that are perceived as fair by the larger number of diverse and specialized employees. As firms grow in size, they hire increasingly specialized technical staff and increasingly professional managers. This trend deepens insight in areas that complement staff expertise, particularly business insight brought by those who manage corporate engineers and scientists. When implemented effectively, organizational standards provide a sense of rationality and focus for the firm and the individuals within it—a sense of what can be expected as a career path and of positional outcomes for contributing in a reasonably well-defined and mutually understood way.

In a great many respects and situations, the formalization, structure, and specialization of management practice described above benefits mature firms. Costs are reduced as economies of scale and scope are realized with standardized policies, and employees understand their roles in the organization and can adjust their actions to align their efforts and contributions to the firm's strategy. Uncertainties about who is responsible for doing what are decreased. However, as a result of formalized procedures, managerial decision-making about resources and support, organizational position, and even appropriate career paths may grow increasingly detached from individualized needs. At best, these decisions may be based on quantifiable criteria associated with the general expectations for one's functional domain (such as number of patents, if one is a research and development [R&D] scientist) and, at worst, on managerial preference that may not be tied directly to long-run firm success (i.e., whether the manager perceives one as a "team player").

By their very nature, formal management policies address the needs, concerns, and capabilities of the "average" or typical employee as opposed to the "exception" or "exemplar." This strategy may leave little discretionary latitude for managers to address and support the needs and capabilities of individuals who contribute to the corporation unconventionally, such as our Serial Innovators. As noted in previous chapters, these individuals differ enormously from average employees. Organizational decisions about exemplar individuals may need to be based on personal insight about their potential for contribution, which grows out of a relationship characterized by connectedness and understanding. In the extreme, we observe a Dilbert-esque situation with evil Catbert-like human resource directors and clueless "Pointy-Haired Bosses" determining the fate of insightful, yet helpless, employees.

The questions, then, are when and to what extent are we to expect management and the organization to adapt to meet the needs of an individual? To what extent is it the Serial Innovator's responsibility to reach out to management and the organization? Consider the following story.

MANAGING SERIAL INNOVATORS:
ONE MANAGER'S SOLUTION

Shung Wu "Andy" Lee was a professor of electrical engineering at the University of Illinois, and a world leader in applying novel computational science techniques for rapid modeling and simulation of radar signatures, when he founded Defense Electromagnetics Company (DEMACO) in 1986. The technologies he developed allow, for example, real-time identification of aircraft as either friend or foe by U.S. Air Force pilots. After the company was successfully established and growing, Andy hired Dennis Andersh, a former U.S. Air Force customer of DEMACO's whom Andy had known and respected for several years, as president in 1995. Dennis's mandate was to position the company for further growth and then sale. DEMACO's sale to Science Applications International Corporation (SAIC) was completed in 1998. Andy, having satisfied his ambitions for what was now SAIC-DEMACO, retired in 2002.

SAIC is a Fortune 500 scientific, engineering, and technology applications company that uses deep domain knowledge, like that created by Andy Lee and his team of technologists, to solve problems of vital importance in national security, energy, the environment, critical infrastructure, and health care. Currently, its subsidiaries have approximately forty-five thousand employees and offices in more than 150 cities worldwide. SAIC "solves our customers' mission-critical problems with innovative applications of technology and expertise" (www.saic.com). In the case of the former DEMACO unit, that expertise has to do with novel computational science techniques. DEMACO's primary customer is the U.S. government, especially the Department of Defense and Homeland Security.

SAIC, a conglomeration of small companies, is structured to create ongoing technology development and innovation in its decentralized units. Headquarters sets financial and growth goals for individual units, but allows business units to operate relatively independently and entrepreneurially when deciding how to meet those goals. Organizing the company as a set of smaller, self-contained units allows each to react nimbly to the environment as they see fit—at least in theory. SAIC also permits units to compete among each other for the same customers, believing that this competition fosters more rapid technological advances as various business units try to solve the same problem using different technology approaches. The corporate belief is that this loose structure—with everyone trying to solve customers' problems—coupled with employee ownership, enables SAIC to thrive and remain technically current.

In spite of such intentional organizational free-market design, the transition from independent DEMACO entity to SAIC business unit led to decreased, rather than increased, innovation for the group. Two aspects of how SAIC operates specifically contributed to this problem. First, SAIC organizationally "stovepipes" (SAIC's term) or silos different functional groups, as do many large firms, for operational and managerial efficiency. Developers from different technical subspecialties formally report to different group leaders, who in turn each report to an overall lab director. When DEMACO was an independent company, there was no lab hierarchy. Andy and Dennis knew what all of the roughly thirty employees were doing. Everyone interacted with each other directly, so that there was shared knowledge of the origins of new, good ideas and of the strong contributors in the organization. Teams assembled and disassembled across the different subfunctional specialties as needed to create new solutions to customers' problems. Two years after the DEMACO subsidiary had created the functional domain stovepipes and more hierarchical structure, mirroring the way the rest of SAIC was structured, creativity appeared to fade. The stovepipes were stifling the cross-function fertilization necessary for rapidly pushing technology development.

The second factor impeding innovation was SAIC's revenue model. As the majority of SAIC's business units are either service provider or software development units, SAIC's revenue model is based on "time sold to customers," similar to the revenue model of law firms. However, this model decreased the latitude for investing discretionary time and funds into new breakthrough technology solutions and product concepts. In order to meet near-term financial goals, the firm emphasized direct contract work, as opposed to internal R&D. Dennis was not seeing new technologies coming out of the technical staff; they were just applying technical band-aids and making repairs to existing products. Nothing new and creative was available to catch customers' or potential customers' interest or to allow the unit to expand into new solution areas.

As these new realities emerged, Dennis responded in two significant ways. Dennis re-recruited Andy, the Serial Innovator behind DEMACO's early success, back into the organization. Andy has been back in SAIC's former DEMACO unit ever since, identifying and creating next-generation business opportunities. Dennis also separated the division into two organizations: one "stovepiped" organization to focus on incremental product development and support, and another designed to focus on new technology development. For developing new technologies, he created a small cross-functional incubator organization, with Andy Lee as its innovating focus. He colocated the most technically competent people in the business unit into this incubator—relocating a number of them from elsewhere across the country—and let them "create new juices" that would help feed the rest of the organization. All those recruited into the group were other Serial Innovators like Andy or proven technologists from the different disciplines that Andy and the other Serial Innovators might need as technical support.

Andersh believed that avoiding the bureaucracy that emerges naturally in large, mature firms was essential for the group. Thus, the incubator organization was nonhierarchical, with very few constraints except for the mandate to create new technologies that would grow sales in new areas to current customers and would bring in new customers. The incubator team would gather for daylong working sessions every few weeks. The tasks at these working sessions were to share understanding about customers, customer needs, market trends, and the technology knowledge residing within the team and elsewhere in the world. They would brainstorm ideas and work through tough technical issues. The group jointly worked to figure out how to make technologies and concepts more useful and to flesh ideas out more fully, or would decide to abandon a current approach or concept and start over with entirely new ideas. Between the meetings, the individual technologists, led by Andy, would delve into specific issues more fully, and then bring the results of their efforts—whether breakthrough or bust—back into the next working group. As with other Serial Innovators, Andy would lead the final development of the breakthrough products and help customers implement the solutions.

About a year later, Andy and the small incubator group, with their cross-functional approach to technology development, was generating three times the revenue that it cost to support it—and more new revenue than the rest of the unit combined! However, the investment level on future products is difficult to sustain; supporting today's businesses too often demands the best talent. Even the good managers of innovation succumb to the pressures to deliver results immediately. And sure enough, as the new product growth created by the team required resources to be applied to the near-term needs of the business, members of the group were moved back into the parts of the organization that supported and updated current products. Over time, the incubator team slowly dissolved. Still, Dennis intends to reestablish the incubator group every few years as an ongoing mechanism to create the next generation of new technologies that the division needs to obtain new customers.

Talking with Dennis about his unit and staff reveals the depth of relational insight he has about managing high-impact Serial Innovators, as evidenced in the words he uses in his description of Andy:

[C]reative; personable; driven; ambition; the desire to do something that has an impact; actually build something; build something that somebody's actually going to use; applications-driven; good man/good person . . . creative vision; tenacity; unwilling to give up, no matter how difficult the problems are; collaborative;

cooperative; good teacher; got a vision; passion; he wants to go after it, and I can't fault him for that . . . studies and reads a lot; good listener; listens to the customer's problem; goes off and does the research and comes up with possible solutions; can probe and ask questions; had to staff him recently on a whole new business area—two days later he had a solution; kindness; dedication to get the job done in a timely and cost-efficient manner . . . comes up with the vision and he implements it into a solution; he keeps pecking around the edges; he pecks at it another way, and it may not end up exactly how he thought it'd end up.

These insights reflect how he manages current Serial Innovators, as well as how he identifies and develops the next generation of Serial Innovators. Dennis understands how his incubator staff of Serial Innovators and their support team differ from the typical development team, and how his role is different from that of managing incremental innovation.

Dennis describes the freedom he provides these individuals as "taking off the handcuffs." He finds the "right" people—those who mirror the descriptions of Serial Innovators presented in the previous chapters—and provides them the space to work creatively outside the normal bureaucracy of a mature firm. He minimizes their constraints, but charges them to look at problems from a broader perspective, to be visionary, and to create new technologies that can be developed into product concepts that solve customer problems better than any other available solution. Rather than assigning them to tasks for which he can bill out their services to customers now, he provides them with the funds necessary to attain their objective from profits derived elsewhere in the organization, taking a personal risk that their efforts will eventually result in new revenue streams. As he puts it, "I kind of said—'here's the money, go do it' and left them alone."

Having said this, Dennis doesn't leave this innovation team entirely alone. He conducts regular project reviews with his Serial Innovators, getting insight as to what's going on and looking for ways that he may adjust the activity or encourage deeper investigation if the case warrants. He understands how to tether himself to his Serial Innovators without tying them too tightly. He acknowledges the value of deadlines and also knows that a time constraint on invention can inhibit innovative thought processes. He understands that he must be as flexible as possible in both setting and adjusting time constraints, knowing that, in the end, it is a delivered product and financial return that matters.

Dennis protects his top Serial Innovator, Andy, by freeing him of administrative responsibility. When Andy is in pursuit of a vision, he specifically doesn't want to do what he refers to as "j work"—a term he derives from his field of computational electromagnetics. In Andy's field, every number has a real part and an imaginary part, and the imaginary part is denoted by the symbol j. Andy wants always to focus on the real work—innovating—not on what he sees as "imaginary work," such as attending staff meetings, managing others in the group, and worrying about budgets. To get the most from Andy, Dennis releases him from j-type managerial responsibilities and allows him to focus on breakthrough product development.

Dennis also understands the inherent value of giving Serial Innovators regular customer exposure and interaction: informal, one-on-one interaction that permits them to gain new insight and to present their ideas openly. He sees that customer and Serial Innovator alike are pleased with such interactions—the customer appreciates knowing where things are headed, and the Serial Innovator gains sufficient autonomy to understand customer needs firsthand.

More formal reward systems also are part of Dennis's management tool kit. First, he acknowledges that SAIC's employee ownership structure enables alignment between day-to-day employee actions and personal financial rewards. Moreover, the Serial Innovators in his unit are eligible to receive significant stock awards that, with multiyear vesting, serve to retain these rare individuals.

In a nutshell, Dennis "gets it" when it comes to managing breakthrough Serial Innovators. And the increased profits for his unit within SAIC demonstrate the value of having managers who know how to manage Serial Innovators effectively.

This vignette illustrates the three aspects essential to successfully managing Serial Innovators: teaching managers how to support creativity through their own informal, relational management practices; helping managers understand how these rare employees respond to more formal management practices; and placing Serial Innovators where they have the support and latitude to work the way they need to work.

INFORMAL, RELATIONAL CARING
FOR SERIAL INNOVATORS

The individualistic needs of Serial Innovators are perhaps best met through the informal management practices of their immediate supervisors. Whereas most standard (formal) human resources policies are implemented to treat individuals in the organization equally for equal performance, the informal management practices of direct supervisors can be customized for each individual's special needs and can be applied differentially depending on performance. When informal management is practiced poorly, the Serial Innovator's needs are not sufficiently understood, and his or her potential is squandered. This is not to suggest that every person in the organization should receive individualized treatment or accommodation, opportunities, or rewards. If the cost of this effort for an individual is higher than the return from that individual, such accommodation is unnecessary or even wasteful. When the return is significant—as we have seen in the case of Serial Innovators—such individualized accommodation is essential and profitable.

In thinking about how to individualize informal management, managers must remember that, first and foremost, Serial Innovators are intrinsically *and* extrinsically motivated to create breakthrough innovations (Chapter 5). They are intrinsically motivated by the joy of discovery, by the innovation task itself; they are extrinsically motivated by external circumstances—specifically by seeing customers' lives change and improve through using the products the Serial Innovator has created. This tendency contrasts with previous findings in the creativity literature, which suggest that extrinsic rewards quash creativity and that the most creative individuals are those who are inherently motivated to be creative, and who create because they just have to for themselves (Amabile 1988). Though partially motivated by extrinsic rewards, Serial Innovators' extrinsic motivators differ from previous conceptions of what constitutes an extrinsic motivator (concrete rewards such as increased pay and bonuses).

To be precise, Serial Innovators are intrinsically motivated to solve problems that are important to customers, and this weighs heavily on how they are best managed. They passionately want to see their ideas become a commercial reality, to see people using and benefiting from the innovations they have conceived, developed, and taken to market. Although they may welcome or accept increased pay and bonuses, as we explain below, these are not their primary motivators.

In addition, their managers must keep in mind that Serial Innovators intrinsically thrive on working at the leading edges of technology to solve tough, complex problems. Even when undertaking such challenges, as discussed in Chapter 5, Serial Innovators are *pragmatically idealistic*. They want what is right for all parties. For their customers, they want a product that addresses needs and solves problems. For their firms, they want to make a significant financial impact by producing an oversize return on the (long-term) investment that has been made in them and their development efforts. For their colleagues, they want an opportunity to work jointly on important problems and revel in the success of their efforts. And for themselves, they want the opportunity to innovate over and over again, and fair treatment (reward) when their breakthrough new products succeed in the marketplace.

The nature of the *innovation processes* that Serial Innovators use greatly impacts how they are best managed. As discussed in Chapter 2, Serial Innovators spend considerable time identifying problems worthy of their efforts and then invest significantly more time deeply understanding these problems. They chew on important, complex problems—on their own and with other, trusted colleagues—over extended periods of time, digesting various clues, leads, and insights, seeing an emerging collective, innovative new whole. Taking together their motivation and the processes they use, we see that Serial Innovators are driven to make breakthrough innovation happen for large, mature firms. Yet, such breakthrough innovation by its very nature requires time, financial investment, specialized resources, and technically competent colleagues. Thus, while everything is aligned *within* these individuals to succeed (both intrinsic and extrinsic motivations), not everything is necessarily *organizationally* available for them to succeed.

So, then, what are the management implications of these observations? The most critical implication is that the Serial Innovator's immediate technical manager has the greatest external influence on the Serial Innovator's ability to be successful through his or her control of resources and time, and that this manager does not need to "drive" the Serial Innovator to produce. Instead, the role of the manager is to unleash and enable the Serial Innovator—in many respects, to let the birds fly!—while providing him or her with a sheltered nest to come home to roost in while incubating their innovations. The best managers provide Serial Innovators with the resources they need and an environment and culture within which they can excel at innovating.

The most effective managers provide the time that Serial Innovators need to deeply understand: to define the most important problems and to see the best solutions to those problems. They do so, variously, by:

1. Understanding that their innovation process will start off with a long period of time in which it looks as if nothing is being done;

2. Having patience with and trust in the Serial Innovator and his/her process;

3. Running interference with more senior levels of management;

4. Not burdening the Serial Innovator with inappropriately bureaucratic tasks; and

5. Not requiring daily or weekly written reports of progress.

Effective managers of Serial Innovators allow them to "fly under the radar" for significant periods of time. However, setting the appropriate output expectation time frame is the real challenge that managers have. This judgment is challenging to develop, so unfortunately, most managers opt for requiring results sooner rather than later, because few senior executives will question that decision. Many senior executives, however, will question the long-term, patient decisions because they take more time to unfold and they are less certain. Thus, managers of Serial Innovators need to develop mechanisms to protect their Serial Innovators from senior executives' impatient demands.

One mechanism managers use to protect Serial Innovators is to manage meetings with senior executives themselves, freeing the Serial Innovator from nonessential bureaucratic responsibilities. Other managers keep the Serial Innovator's projects "off the books" for as long as possible. Sometimes, a word from an important customer to a senior executive is enough to shield the Serial Innovator and provide him or her with the additional time they need to understand and invent.

In addition to time, the most successful managers provide the resources necessary to enable breakthrough innovation. According to one manager, "that was [my Serial Innovator's] only request—'give me the resources to do it.'" These resources may include, but may not be limited to:

- Funds for supplies, specialized equipment, and travel to customer sites and conferences;

- Technically outstanding, team-oriented colleagues who stimulate the Serial Innovator's thinking and who collaborate to make things happen;

- Access to resources elsewhere in the firm, such as pilot manufacturing facilities; and

- Access to other technical experts outside of the organization and firm.

An unusual example of the types of resources a manager may have to come up with occurred when one Serial Innovator was challenged by executive management to shorten significantly the commercialization time of his breakthrough innovation, which had not yet moved from virtual to physical form. To help him address the speed problem, his manager assembled twenty-two of the firm's technical specialists from a number of diverse disciplines for a two-and-a-half-day workshop, which focused on reducing the project's development time. Before the workshop, the Serial Innovator had been convinced the goal was impossible; by the end of the workshop, he saw real potential to shorten the timeline by at least nine months. All it took was one manager enlisting fifty-five person-days of valuable technical resources to aid him in the task.

It is imperative that a Serial Innovator's ability to travel is not hampered, even when the rest of the firm's employee travel budgets are cut or eliminated. Managers of Serial Innovators find creative ways to continue supporting travel, especially travel related to customer immersion. Some firms, such as 3M, have special project or start-up funds to which individuals can apply for funding. Some managers elect to quietly shift budget from other projects (possibly slowing them down) to the Serial Innovator's budget. Other managers use the personal relationships they have with senior executives to obtain additional funding for the Serial Innovator's projects over and above the normal group budget. The salient point here is that, if a Serial Innovator indicates that she/he needs to travel to a customer or a convention at which customers will be found, his or her manager needs to "find" the funding to allow it to happen.

Contrary to the picture that may appear to be emerging, the best managers of Serial Innovators do not merely "take orders" from or "let go" of their Serial Innovator partner. Instead, they find subtle but clear ways to encourage and challenge the Serial Innovator, such as giving them the most difficult and highest-potential problem on which to work. They give Serial Innovators problems that others have not been able to solve. Such managers do not meddle inappropriately or dictate direction to the Serial Innovator—these actions can sour the motivation of most Serial Innovators. Similarly, managers are not absent. They engage Serial Innovators with insight, wisdom, and judgment.

So how might we illustrate this engagement between Serial Innovators and their most effective managers? The best managers are not cheerleaders, merely cajoling the Serial Innovator with shallow platitudes that could be said equally of almost any employee. Similarly, the best managers are not drill sergeants, commanding the Serial Innovator's path, nor are they machine operators, impersonally and dispassionately adjusting policies and project timelines without regard for the flexible and dynamic process of innovation. Finally, outstanding managers do not view their relationships with Serial Innovators as simply transactions, where financial compensation is sufficient to motivate them to excellence.

Instead, in many respects, the interaction and relationship between effective managers and Serial Innovators is not unlike that between exceptional ballroom dance partners. Each has their strengths and their own roles. One cannot succeed fully without the other, and each must trust that the other will be where they are supposed to be, when they are supposed to be there, and do what they are supposed to be doing. If one dancer looks good, their partner does as well; the best navigate the floor with agility, flexibility, grace, and beauty—simultaneously as individuals and together, aware of and responding to subtle changes in the tempo and dynamics of the music, as well as to each other's personality. When it works, it is magical, and they dance on and on, sometimes together for years, producing an effect far beyond that which either could attain on their own.

This means that managers who have big egos, need the limelight, or need to be the focus of attention cannot manage Serial Innovators effectively. The most successful managers of Serial Innovators subjugate their own egos to enable the Serial Innovator, and thus their organizations, to succeed.

Susan's technical manager at the paper products firm told us that part of his success in managing Serial Innovators stemmed from his realization, early in his career, that "I'm not capable of solving the vast majority of the problems that the business needs to solve, but that [the business] does have people who *are* capable of solving those problems." After that realization, he decided that his job was to "get the right people in the right spot with the right challenge where they're motivated" to innovate. His preference would be to have Susan, the Serial Innovator who currently works for him, do so for the rest of her organizational life. We heard this sentiment not just from this manager, but also from managers in many different industries. Effective managers do not compete with Serial Innovators; rather they understand that when the Serial Innovators "look good," they as managers "look good." It is a win–win situation when it comes to managing such powerful, high-impact performers.

When a Serial Innovator finds a manager who understands how to manage them effectively, they may end up working for that manager for a long period of time. One Serial Innovator had worked for the same manager for over seventeen years, moving in concert across the organization and up the technology organizational ladder. Another manager in a medical devices firm, Al, has managed Fred, the Serial Innovator who watches nurses for insight (see Chapter 3), for only six years. When Fred started working for Al, their relationship was the typical one for a manager and subordinate: Al was higher in the organizational ladder than Fred, and made more money. Now, because Fred's multiple innovations have brought millions of dollars of revenues and profits to the firm, both men have risen up the organizational ladder and make more money. However, Fred now holds a position two rungs above Al, his manager, and makes significantly more money, in clear violation of extant human resource policies at the firm (much to HR's consternation and disapproval). Al is an excellent example of a manager successfully subjugating his ego to the greater needs of the organization. Both Fred and Al are happy with this reporting arrangement. The senior executives in the firm have decided to keep this arrangement intact because of its effectiveness, rather than moving Fred to reporting to someone higher in the organizational ladder, such as the president of R&D, which would be more in line with human resource policies.

Alternatively, we found that one of the few reasons that a Serial Innovator considers changing jobs or even companies is when they are assigned to a manager who "just doesn't get it," who does not understand how to manage them effectively. Characteristics of managers that drive Serial Innovators to find new managers or change firms include:

1. Micromanaging—dictating *both* the problem and the investigatory path;

2. Being transactional rather than relational—Serial Innovators work for people, not positions or roles;

3. Impatience—expecting the Serial Innovator to dive right into developing solutions before she/he has had the time to understand the problem sufficiently;

4. Being stingy with resources—making the Serial Innovator constantly barter for what he needs; and

5. Taking credit for the Serial Innovator's successes.

Executives need to know who their Serial Innovators are, and to ensure proactively that they are managed by someone who understands their special needs and how to manage them.

In summary, then, the most important factor in successfully managing Serial Innovators is to provide them with managers who understand how to informally manage them as exemplar individuals with needs that differ significantly from those of the typical technologist.

THE INTRIGUING ROLE OF FORMALLY MANAGING SERIAL INNOVATORS

Conspicuously absent in the discussion to this point is any mention of the more *formal* management tools traditionally emphasized in the discussion of employee motivation—salary increases, bonuses, promotions, innovation awards, and other such recognition. Such techniques were regularly identified as salient by both Serial Innovators and their technical managers alike (Hebda et al. 2007). Interestingly, however, although these tools are important to Serial Innovators, they are by no means viewed as being sufficient to successfully motivate and manage them. Instead, we observed that these techniques play a somewhat different role than what one might initially expect, a role that the most successful managers of Serial Innovators understand and master.

Financial rewards, including salary increases, bonuses, and stock options, although deemed important in terms of the purchasing power and security that they bring to Serial Innovators and their families, hold greater symbolic than economic value. Serial Innovators acknowledged that they could make far more money by forming start-up companies to commercialize their breakthrough products. If money had been their primary motivator, then they would have quit their corporations and done just that. However, they chose to give up huge potential financial returns to commercialize their breakthrough innovations in the context of their organizations.

Still, Serial Innovators know that money and profits are the primary measure of success for and within their firms. As sales and profits grow, the firm's stock price climbs, producing shareholder value. The Serial Innovator's logic, then, is that, to the extent that the company's money is shared with them in the form of various types of compensation, the company values their contributions. Money is an indicator that the firm acknowledges and appreciates the Serial Innovator's efforts on its behalf.

Recognition, including patent awards, innovation awards, and admission to corporate technical Fellows' societies, are *retrospectively* deemed very important by Serial Innovators in terms of accurately recognizing what already has been accomplished. Conversely, none of the Serial Innovators we spoke with were effectively motivated by these forms of recognition to contribute more to win such an award. Further, several mentioned the significantly demotivating influence of rewarding the *wrong* people, who actually did not do the work or who actually did not meet the formal guidelines. As pragmatic idealists, such a response from

Serial Innovators should not be surprising. They want what is "right" or "just" for all parties.

Interestingly, when we spoke with triads of Serial Innovators, their direct technical managers, and the human resource managers attached to their business units, we found that the motivational perspectives of the human resource managers differed significantly from that of the Serial Innovators and their technical managers (Hebda et al. 2012). Serial Innovators and their direct technical managers emphasized the importance of the individualized informal motivating role of their direct technical managers; human resource managers repeatedly identified many of the more formal award, reward, and recognition tools (including performance management systems, patent awards, and dual ladder systems) as being the most effective management techniques available. Of special importance to those seeking to effectively manage Serial Innovators, then, is the reality that the human resource function, if not enlightened to the uniqueness of managing Serial Innovators, can represent something of a stumbling block to the type of resource and reward flexibility necessary to successfully manage these exemplar individuals. Human resource managers usually want a "one size fits all" reward, recognition, and personnel management system. Serial Innovators to them are round pegs that do not fit into their personnel policies' square holes. If managers are not careful, then, human resources' standardized policies can actually hinder the flexibility needed to reward and motivate Serial Innovators.

PROVIDING SERIAL INNOVATORS WITH ORGANIZATIONAL SPACE

Christensen (1997) suggests that there is a low likelihood of success when disruptive breakthrough innovations are developed within an existing business unit. His recommendation is, instead, to establish organizations for breakthrough innovation that are entirely separate from existing business units and their need to serve existing customers. Indeed, in the SAIC story, we saw that Dennis Andersh identified the Serial Innovators across his organization (along with the cross-functional personnel needed to support their efforts), and then brought them together into a specialized unit that was then charged with creating new technology-based solutions.

However, this is just one of several structural positions from which Serial Innovators can successfully innovate.

We agree with Christensen that the challenge of supporting breakthrough innovation in large firms is great, but suggest different solutions to overcome the internal barriers to innovation. Missing from Christensen's recommendation is the enormous value that comes from leveraging the resources of a mature firm. Such resources typically are allocated to serve the needs of existing customers; however, we also find value in redistributing some of these funds to facilitate breakthrough innovation. For every case where Christensen's premise has proven to hold, we have observed cases where breakthrough Serial Innovators, teamed with enlightened, involved management, have revitalized the firm. Our position is illustrated graphically in Figure 7.1.

In our research, we observed instances where the internal barriers have been overcome, both by small internal incubator groups, such as the type employed by Dennis Andersh, and by breakthrough Serial Innovators in other organizational structures, as shown in Figure 7.1 and Table 7.1. Serial Innovators located in the bottom right quadrant typically operate within the confines of the R&D group. Serial Innovators in "Liaison" positions typically straddle functional groups, operating with one foot in R&D and the other foot either in marketing or in a position that reports directly to the business unit's executive management. Incubator groups

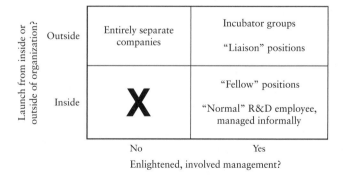

FIGURE 7.1   Comparison and contrast with the recommendations of Christensen (1997)

TABLE 7.1   Alternative organizational choices for locating Serial Innovators

Serial Innovator position	Benefits	Drawbacks
Incubator groups	• Provides focus on the effort • Concentration of intellectual power • Good training/mentoring ground for future Serial Innovators • Economies of scale in support • Only requires one manager who understands Serial Innovators' needs	• Perhaps not sustainable as new business is created that later requires support from individuals in the group • Needs a manager who is not solely measured on current profits
Liaison position sitting between marketing and R&D	• Eliminates administrative responsibilities • Provides high independence for Serial Innovators • Connects marketing, R&D, and strategy	• Requires a great deal of trust in the Serial Innovator • Does not provide supporting personnel that may be needed • Requires a Serial Innovator with exquisite charisma and influencing skills • Likely limited in scope to one Serial Innovator per division
"Fellow" positions	• Provides high independence for Serial Innovators • Eliminates administrative responsibilities • Usually comes with financial support	• Maintaining motivation • Issues of technology transfer • Does not provide supporting personnel that may be needed • Difficulty of staying connected with customers and the business • Strength of role may become diluted if too many are named
"Normal" R&D employee, reporting to a manager and managed informally	• Embeds the Serial Innovator in the organization, giving them easier access to human and equipment resources • May result in long-term stability for supporting the Serial Innovator	• Success depends upon finding or developing a capable manager—and one for each Serial Innovator • Serial Innovator skills at selling and engaging the organization • What happens to the Serial Innovator when his manager retires or leaves the company?

operate independently from R&D or other functional groups, but are still part of the larger organization.

Incubator Groups

As discussed earlier in the chapter, and proposed by other researchers investigating generating breakthrough innovations in mature firms (Liefer et al. 2000; O'Connor et al. 2008), consolidating the division's Serial Innovators into one incubator group charged with developing breakthrough products is one way to structurally position this capability. This structure provides some significant benefits, as identified in Table 7.1. The group has one, and only one, charge: create the next breakthrough innovation(s) for the firm. Given the extreme focus on this effort, everyone in the group clearly understands the firm's expectations of them. This structure also provides concentration of intellectual power in one place and economies of scale for supporting all of the division's Serial Innovators simultaneously. It allows the division to benefit from having multiple Serial Innovators in the organization. It also may provide a place where younger "aspiring" Serial Innovators can more easily learn the breadth of skills they need to grow into full-fledged Serial Innovators. They have role models at hand who can help them learn about the firm's strategy and business in general, teach them how to become immersed in understanding problems deeply and how to talk to customers and potential customers to understand their problems. They also are exposed to technologies peripheral to their primary domains.

As with all organizational structures, however, there are drawbacks to incubator structures. The biggest question associated with this organizational structure is whether it is sustainable over the long run. The breakthrough new technologies taken to market in new products by this group ultimately will need technical support and redevelopment to further improve and refine them over time as the technology matures and customer needs change. Unfortunately, the very best people for those tasks are the technical support people in the incubator group. Thus, as SAIC found, they are likely to be drawn into the "maintain and grow" part of the division to support these products. To keep the incubator functioning, then, the division needs to develop a mechanism to continually introduce other strong technical individuals into the incubator group, perhaps with changing technical expertise, as the Serial Innovators branch into different peripheral technologies. The alternative, of course, is to constitute an incubator group for some period of time, allow it to slowly and naturally dissolve as the new products migrate to other parts of the division, and then to reconstitute it at some later point in time, perhaps with some entirely different technology focus. At issue, then, is what happens to the Serial Innovators who do not want to return to the sustaining parts of the organization? If some mechanism cannot be found to allow them to keep operating as Serial Innovators independently of the incubator group, the firm might lose them to another firm that will allow them to continue to innovate.

The five major keys to successfully using incubators as mechanisms for supporting the division's Serial Innovators are:

1. Colocating the entire group in one physical area;

2. Physically and psychically separating the group from the organization responsible for maintaining and redeveloping the firm's current set of products;

3. Keeping the group attached to the firm's strategy;

4. Finding or developing a manager who understands and knows how to enable and support Serial Innovators; and

5. Sequestering the group from immediate return on investment (ROI) pressures.

Marketing/R&D Liaison Positions

Serial Innovators can also be organizationally situated between marketing and R&D, serving in liaison positions between the two functions. In these positions, Serial Innovators typically report to the VPs (presidents, directors) of marketing and R&D simultaneously, or in some cases, directly to the president of the division or business unit. Reporting directly to the division president provides them with significant organizational legitimization, which may make their influencing job easier. In these positions, Serial Innovators typically are free from administrative responsibilities and can focus all of their time on making connections between the marketing and technology sides of the organization. Because of their formal connections with both functions as well as to senior management, it is easy for them to maintain deep understanding of customer needs, market trends in aggregate, technology developments, and strategy simultaneously.

There are several disadvantages to this structure, however. First, Serial Innovators are exposed: if they don't produce results in some time frame (often arbitrarily defined as "reasonable"), they may lose their standing with upper management. Thus, this organizational structure requires that the senior executives in the division have a great deal of trust in the Serial Innovators. It is likely that only those Serial Innovators with a track record of multiple, significant breakthrough successes can be appointed to these types of positions. In addition, in order for Serial Innovators to function effectively in this organizational situation, they must have credibility with both the marketing and the technical functions, and they must be very highly skilled in obtaining resource support through their own interpersonal capabilities and influencing techniques. Not all Serial Innovators may be as adept politically as is necessary to function in this organizational position, where they have "all the responsibility and none of the authority" to get the job done. Additionally, it is likely that each business unit can support only one Serial Innovator, if this is the structure in which they prefer to situate them organizationally.

"Fellow" Positions

Many firms have created a society or prestigious organization to honor their best technical professionals. Examples include the Victor Mills Society at Proctor & Gamble (P&G; Brunner 2001), the IBM Fellows program (Termin 2002), and 3M's Carlton Society (Nicholson 1998). A number of firms have placed many of their exemplary Serial Innovators into these "Fellow" positions in their R&D organizations. These programs typically are supported at the firm level, rather than at the divisional level. Thus, Serial Innovators in Fellow positions have easier access to other equally competent and creative people from multiple technology and product areas, as the Fellows are likely to be physically colocated in the organization. This organizational structure supports cross-seeding of ideas, which can be critical for breakthrough innovation. These positions most typically grant the Fellows the right to work in whatever technology area they deem interesting and to proceed unfettered by administrative responsibilities. They also typically come with some budget that is solely under the Fellows' control.

Positioning Serial Innovators as Fellows still produces challenges in managing them effectively. The first major challenge is to keep these elite employees intrinsically motivated to continue innovating.* The last thing the firm wants to do is set aside a hugely talented group of individuals who no longer innovate. Fellows (and incubator groups) are charged with creating technologies and products that will move the firm into new white space, helping them transform the firm and grow it beyond the firm's current strategy. However, the breakthrough technologies and products they create likely may not fit into any of the businesses of the current divisions, making it more difficult to get these products transferred out of R&D and into commercial development. As Serial Innovators are highly motivated by seeing customers benefit from using the products and services they have innovated, a history of noncommercialization of the technologies developed by Fellows could adversely impact their intrinsic motivations and hinder future innovations by the group as a whole.

An additional challenge that Fellows may feel is a lack of formal resource support. Fellows need to continue to fully understand their firm's strategy, both individual target market customer needs and aggregate market trends, as well as technology changes and potentialities. Although Fellows positions typically come with research budgets, they do not come with full-blown support staffs. Fellows may have to use their budgets to "buy" time in pilot facilities and to obtain other resource support (people and equipment access) through their own informal networks and their own persuasive capabilities. They may have to make budget trade-offs between maintaining understanding and buying resource support, which may limit their long-term efficiency and effectiveness as Serial Innovators.

The four keys to success in using Fellows positions as the organizational structure for innovations are:

1. Not diluting the honor of the position by appointing too many Fellows;

2. Giving Fellows formal access to support staff (scientists, engineers, and technicians) and equipment;

3. Providing Fellows with sufficient budgets to allow them to innovate and take projects to physical confirmation; and

4. Keeping Fellows attached to strategy.

---

* This is akin to the issue of keeping professors in academia research-active and research-productive after tenure.

Revisit: Managing Serial Innovators as "Typical" R&D Employees Using Informal Techniques

Liaison and Fellow positions are organizational structures that can only be used for already-proven Serial Innovators. These are post hoc declarations of an individual's success at repeatedly developing breakthrough innovations. There are only two organizational ways in which individuals can become Serial Innovators: through mentoring by other, established Serial Innovators in incubator organizations, and through their informal management as a "typical" R&D employee reporting to a "typical" R&D manager. As incubator groups for fostering breakthrough innovations are rare, the vast majority of upcoming and "proving" Serial Innovators will end up being managed informally in the R&D organization (in addition to having a number, perhaps the majority, of proven Serial Innovators also being managed in this way). It is thus imperative for R&D managers to deeply understand these exemplar individuals and how to identify, develop, and then manage them.

Choosing Organizational Structure(s) for Your Firm

The key is that, at some point, all of the exemplary Serial Innovators we studied found one or more enlightened managers who enabled their activity in various organizational forms. On the one hand, all organizations that want to take advantage of the unique capabilities of Serial Innovators will have to have at least some individually enlightened managers who know how to manage Serial Innovators informally and potential Serial Innovators effectively, within the realm of the "typical" R&D structure, management processes, and HR policies. On the other hand, firms may also want to think about whether other organizational structure(s) also may be useful to help them more formally manage both upcoming and proven Serial Innovators. Firms may find one or another of the structures more appropriate, based on the firm's culture. Table 7.2 may help firms determine which organizational form(s) may be most appropriate for them.

Across the firms in which we investigated breakthrough innovation, after informal management capabilities, the most frequently used structure we found for managing already-proven Serial Innovators was the Fellow system. The least frequently used structure was the incubator organization,

TABLE 7.2 Characteristics of organizational structures for Serial Innovators

	Incubator groups	Liaison positions	Fellow positions	"Normal" R&D employee
Serial Innovator type	Proven and developing	Proven	Proven	Proven and developing
Management responsibility	Individual manager plus Serial Innovators as mentors	Individual manager or joint management (2)	Diffuse: no direct individual manager?	Individual manager
Management level	Division director or VP	Division VP or president	HQ VP	Functional manager, director
Serial Innovator risk	Exposure shared with group manager	Highly exposed	Little personal exposure	Exposure ceded to manager

and informal management in R&D was a bit more frequently seen than the liaison structure. However, our sample by no means provides statistical support for the relative frequency that these structures are actually used, and may not represent the general population of firms.

Even firms with liaison or Fellow structures will need to have in place some mechanism for developing upcoming Serial Innovators. Liaison positions may be most useful for firms with strong functional silos, in which there is little direct communication between marketing and R&D. The liaison Serial Innovator then helps overcome those functional silos. However, these also may be the organizations that will find it hardest to implement, unless the position is decreed by the president of the division and the Serial Innovator reports directly to him or her, rather than jointly to the two VPs. It is likely that only firms with large, central R&D staffs will be able to create Fellow positions for their Serial Innovators; firms in which R&D is decentralized to the business unit level likely will not be able to implement this structure. Finally, Serial Innovators will be at highest personal risk in incubator groups and liaison positions. These structures may be most appropriate, then, in firms that do not penalize new product failure, but that deem failure to be a natural part of trying to develop breakthrough products as well as something to be used as a learning point.

MANAGING SERIAL INNOVATORS IN
CONTRAST TO OTHER R&D EMPLOYEES

In some respects, the discussion to this point begs the question, "Who gets this special treatment?" That is, who should, or should not, be given the time and resources to explore new product concepts while being gently tethered to their manager, and why?

We begin by reviewing the new product development (NPD) roles outlined in Chapter 1 (see Figure 1.5 and Table 1.2): Inventor, Champion, Implementer, and the role-transcending Serial Innovator. In order to understand how management can most effectively interact with each of these roles, and how those interactions must by their very nature differ, we must first further unpack how the Inventor-Champion-Implementer scenario of NPD differs from the Serial Innovator scenario.

In many respects, the Inventor-Champion-Implementer scenario represents a "filter" view of innovation. The Inventor generates a great number of ideas or potential technology solutions, followed by the filtering of opportunity recognition conducted by the Champion. Only those technologies for which the Champion foresees significant market and financial potential are carried toward new product launch—through the additional successive filters of the Stage-Gate® or other formal product development process—by the Implementer(s). In contrast, as we have discussed in Chapter 2, Serial Innovators instead refine inventive ideas into new products as illustrated in the hourglass model, revisiting not only their understanding of the need, but also the importance of the problem itself all along the development path. In doing so, Serial Innovators successively focus their concepts toward a successful product launch. The managerial implications of these two differing perspectives are significant.

Serial Innovators have all the capabilities needed for developing successful breakthrough products, residing in conjunction with a motivation that invention and innovation are a means to provide customers with better solutions to their problems and to earn the firm profits. This perspective supports the idea of "letting the birds fly" in managing Serial Innovators. Inventors, in contrast, are primarily idea generators and technology solution providers. If allowed to operate without guidance and direction from the marketplace, such individuals may develop into "profitless prolifics," generating one new patentable technology after another without any profitable application and, therefore, without any financial return. Inventors' skills and inclinations may lead them in a direction that may not be compatible with corporate goals. In practice, the most successful Inventors are given fairly specific problems on which to work and at times are teamed with those able to fill the Champion and Implementer roles. Someone other than the Inventor takes responsibility for suggesting the technology path that may ultimately lead to a profitable new product, and someone else also takes responsibility for seeing the connection between a customer problem and a potential technology solution.

Another way to think about managing these different types of individuals is based on whether they use managerial, strategic, or effectual thinking in the way they approach innovation (Sarasvathy 2001). Managerial thinking selects among known means to achieve a particular goal. These decisions constitute the day-to-day way in which the firm is run. Champions look at the ideas and concepts that R&D has produced and determine which idea(s) match the business unit's goals. Managers need to make sure that Champions understand the firm's goals and have access to the R&D personnel who are developing technology solutions. Strategic thinking, on the other hand, generates new means to achieve a goal. Some Inventors approach innovation strategically, most often when they are given the goal to invent by upper management, such as senior management in R&D. In practice, we find that some Inventors, however, do not invent strategically to specific goals, which is when they are most likely to create technologies that do not produce profits for the firm. The most effective R&D Inventors are those who are given specific (perhaps difficult and complex) technical goals that more senior managers have taken the responsibility for linking to the firm's overall strategy and then given them the technical freedom to figure out how to invent to meet those technical goals.

Finally, effectual thinking imagines possible new ends using a set of means. This is how Serial Innovators approach innovation; they solve new customer problems, innovating to a new goal and using whatever means they need to do so. When a particular technical path does not seem to be working, they modify the path to get to the end goal. These Serial Innovators, then, like Champions, need to understand fully the firm's long-term strategy. They need also to understand how the firm's strategy trajectory may evolve in the future, in order to imagine "possible new ends." While still working at the mid-levels of the organization, they need significant exposure to upper-level strategic thinking, whereas Inventors typically do not. Executive management provides the strategic ends to Inventors. In addition, Serial Innovators, like Inventors, need the freedom to find the means that will get them to the new ends. However, because the ends are likely to be more nebulous and business-oriented than those more technical and concrete ends given to Inventors, Serial Innovators are likely to need significantly more freedom, in terms of time and different types of resources, to innovate successfully.

Thus, it is important for good managers to distinguish those who get freedom and enabling support from those who don't—not as punishment, but because some R&D personnel are capable of moving past technical strategic thinking to effectual business thinking, and others may not be capable of or interested in doing so. This selection process demands that managers evaluate their employees to find the right fit into the innovation process roles for each person and to provide opportunities for individual development that align with what they will need in that role.

BARRIERS TO MASTERING THE MANAGEMENT OF SERIAL INNOVATORS AND WAYS TO OVERCOME THEM

We have begun to believe that the only thing rarer than Serial Innovators are managers who are able to identify and nurture Serial Innovators, and who can take advantage of what these employees have to offer an organization. There are many valid reasons for the lack of managerial abilities, including, but not limited to, the following:

1. Because of public firm ownership and market incentives, most managers are more worried about today's operations, next quarter's results, and the optimization of the current business than they are about the possibilities available in the more uncertain future (when the manager may not even still be working at the firm).

2. Senior managers believe the most important business elements to understand are budgets, schedules, financial impact, and markets. They rarely attempt to understand the technical issues and trade-offs, leaving this to R&D managers.

3. Managerial time and attention are in short supply.

4. Managers strive to understand in order to decide. Serial Innovators strive to understand in order to master and then create; they need to bring something into existence that never was.

5. In the worst case, some managers view their roles as competing with those of the technical staff in their organizations.

Rarely will managers, even R&D managers, be able to master technologies, especially multiple technologies simultaneously, at the level of depth associated with any of the Serial Innovators we have studied. So what should we expect? Following are four possible actions that could help managers better understand the issues associated with managing Serial Innovators.

Demonstrate a Willingness to Learn

Due to time limits, there is no way any individual can be knowledgeable about everything. The issue is what level of understanding—understanding in order to engage or to more deeply make connections—is helpful in managing Serial Innovators. Managers of Serial Innovators only need to be able to engage them in substantive discourse during the innovation process. The Serial Innovators are the ones who must understand to make connections, not their managers. Managers have to be able to keep up, at least on some level. Some managers find that a modicum of individual reading and study on a topic is sufficient to understand where their Serial Innovators are going, and make time for such supplementary endeavors. Other managers prefer to attend a conference for a few days, obtaining understanding by immersing themselves in a particular domain for a concentrated dose of learning. Still others use the Serial Innovator him- or herself—they may schedule frequent, purposeful lunches where the Serial Innovator presents a tutorial to the manager on a prearranged topic. Whatever the method, Serial Innovators prefer managers who show their support for them by demonstrating a willingness to learn about the new areas into which the Serial Innovator is delving.

Employ Multiple Engagement Methods

Managers' biases toward action and decision-making are often contrary to the methods needed to engage Serial Innovators. Bill Hewlett was said to have an engagement approach with engineers that entailed three types of reviews. The first engagement method was one of curiosity and enthusiasm for the Serial Innovator and for the work being done. His curiosity indicated how important the Serial Innovator's work was to him as a manager personally, and to the organization. In addition, this engagement method can help the manager understand where the Serial Innovator is heading, and what related preparation might be done to better relate to the Serial Innovator. The second engagement method focused on understanding what learning the engineer had achieved and challenging the engineer to make business connections. In this engagement method, the manager demonstrates to the Serial Innovator his or her belief in the importance of the project by putting effort into understanding the problem and/or solution at hand. The third engagement method focused on making a decision about whether to continue investing in the project. For simple projects, one of these methods may suffice. However, for most of the complex projects that Serial Innovators undertake, multiple iterations across the methods will be necessary. Furthermore, even within iterating among methods, a manager may have to go back to the Serial Innovator multiple times to increase his or her understanding of the project (the second method) before sufficient information has been shared to allow a decision to be made.

Betting on People

Several Serial Innovators described events where their jobs were on the line—moments when at least some set of managers did not believe in them, their ideas, or their ability to deliver. Their innovations would never have seen the marketplace or been successful unless some manager somewhere in the organization ultimately had been willing to support something risky that challenged prevailing beliefs and experiences. If Serial Innovators come back after having been told no, listen to them and bet on them.

Coming back after rejection takes a high level of commitment to an idea and a strong belief that they are right—pay attention! People are exactly what experienced venture capital companies bet on—the management team, the people proposing the new company or technology, not necessarily the proposed product. Smart managers of Serial Innovators employ the same people-based bets.

Understand and Diagnose Whether the Innovation Represents a Structural Shift or a Paradigm Change*

Structural shifts are based on technology capability. For example, the move from transistors to semiconductors was a technological structural shift. Paradigm changes are the change in mind-set often associated with structural shifts. The move to decentralized personal computing from centralized mainframe computing was a paradigm shift resulting from the structural shift to semiconductors. Although we typically think of Serial Innovators as enabling structural shifts, they actually work in either or both domains. Structural shifts are more factual and data-driven. Paradigm changes are based on facts that are interpreted differently into a new way of working or thinking. Because the Serial Innovator's interpretations usually contradict how the majority view the same data, paradigm changes are more challenging and more likely to produce significant conflict in an organization. Managers need to ask if there may be structural shifts or paradigm changes associated with those data and prepare to manage the organization differentially for those changes.

All four of these practices will help managers overcome the firm's impatience with the time and effort required to create breakthrough innovations, while demonstrating their support for the Serial Innovator's project through personal effort and engagement.

---

* Charles H. House, executive director, Media X at Stanford University, personal communication with R. Price.

8   LOVE LETTERS TO
OUR CUSTOMERS*
*Serial Innovators, Aspiring Serial Innovators,
and All Those with and for Whom They Work*

Serial Innovators exist in many organizations. They represent a "personal perspective" for innovating that exists above and beyond the "process perspective" that has become the standard by which firms innovate. That is, rather than the formal, standardized "process" driving new product development (NPD), resulting predominantly in a stream of incremental offerings brought to market very efficiently and effectively, individuals drive innovation, seeking new solutions to important problems that customers have. However, Serial Innovators are not a silver bullet. They will not fix all of the firm's innovation problems. They are not a replacement for normal product development efforts that support the ongoing business. They do, however, provide an additional, and potentially highly effective, mechanism for supporting organic growth of the firm.

Although small in terms of overall numbers, Serial Innovators have an organizational impact that greatly exceeds the frequency with which they appear. Hundreds of millions of dollars of profit have accrued to Alberto Culver, Caterpillar, Procter & Gamble (P&G), and Hewlett-Packard (HP)/

---

* We found Tom Osborn's characterization of his products being "love letters to women" so compelling that we just couldn't help stealing his phrase to try and convey, once again, the power behind having a passion to do something.

Agilent just from the products that the four named Serial Innovators profiled in this book have invented and commercialized. Thus, organizations that know how to identify, develop, manage, and support Serial Innovators will improve their probability of generating significant revenue and profit growth from moving into new white spaces, even as technological paradigms shift and disruptive innovation occurs in an industry.

We believe that Serial Innovators have the potential to exist in all organizations. Nonetheless, identifying, developing, and managing Serial Innovators requires special managerial skills and deep relational insights. Becoming a Serial Innovator is not easy, being a Serial Innovator is not easy, managing Serial Innovators is not easy, and developing a culture in the organization that can support Serial Innovators is not easy. However, all this can be done, and there is great potential for your organization if you can create a haven in which Serial Innovators can effectively innovate.

The next several pages contain our "love letters" to the firm's creators (Serial Innovators, potential or aspiring Serial Innovators); colleagues of Serial Innovators; students in science, technology, engineering, and mathematics still preparing at universities; managers (the Serial Innovator's technical and human resources managers); and executives (the senior technical executive and senior business executive).

Each of these love letters address the following six topics, customized for each customer of this book identified above:

1. Our *Hopes* for what this book has done for you—what new information, realizations, and motivations it has brought to you;

2. Our *Fears* of what may be impeding you from being/becoming/working with or managing Serial Innovators;

3. Our *Challenge* to you on how to improve what you are now doing;

4. The *Blessing* that we believe will result, should you rise to our challenges;

5. The *Curse* that likely will result, should you ignore or not be able to rise to our challenges; and

6. Our *Dream* for what the outcome from rising to our challenges will be to each audience and/or to the firm.

Rising to the challenges presented in the following pages will be difficult. However, we *promise* that making the recommended efforts will be worth it, to each of you personally, to the firm, and most important, to your customers. By meeting these challenges, you will have contributed greatly to the lives of many, both inside and outside of the organization. We strongly believe that Serial Innovators represent another mechanism, in addition to technology push and market pull pathways, for creating breakthrough innovation. If there is any way in which we can help you or your firm, please do not hesitate to contact us.

Respectfully submitted,
Abbie   abbie.griffin@business.utah.edu
Ray   price1@illinois.edu
Bruce   bvojak@illinois.edu

Dear Serial Innovators:

We started along this research path because we noticed that some individuals in corporations just seemed to bring game-changing, breakthrough new products to market over and over again, and we were curious about just how you did that. Along the way, we've been privileged to meet and interview a stunning set of individuals just like you. We know the great impact you have had and can have again. With this book, we publicly honor your accomplishments and thank you for making our lives better.

Hope
Our hope is that this book encouraged you to persevere in your innovating path, and that you saw yourself, your colleagues, your customers, and your management in the various stories we shared. We also hope that the research pointed out to you: (1) specific additional actions you can undertake to increase your effectiveness as a Serial Innovator, and (2) additional domains (technical, business, and interpersonal) for improving your already superlative ability to "discern" based on experiential intuition. We hope that the techniques and examples described in this book will help you take your abilities to their "next level"— whatever level that might be—so that your desire to solve important customer problems by creating new products will be realized, valued, and rewarded.

Fear
We recognize the challenges presented to you who attempt to implement breakthrough innovation within large, mature firms. Our fear is that the obstacles may become so great that you lose heart, commitment, or focus. There will likely be a temptation to change organizations after frustration begins to build, in the hope of finding an organization that supports you. However, unless you persist in your current organization until you do all you can politically, you ultimately will fail in the next organization, as well. Our fear is that you may give up too soon—don't!

Challenge

Our challenge, then, is that you continue to study intently the subtleties of customer needs and of navigating the firm's politics, and that you continue to demonstrate courage in serving customer and company alike. You must accept the fact that deeply understanding customer needs—that is, customer immersion—is a "white space" task in the organization, for which no one really takes responsibility other than you, the Serial Innovator, for doing in depth.

"Blessing"

If you rise to our challenges, you will either succeed by navigating your organization or slowly come to realize that certain factors are missing in the organization that cannot be overcome. Thus, you will either continue to bring new insights to market as breakthrough products or will have the confidence to move on to more fruitful organizational settings.

"Curse"

If you do not rise to our challenges, you will wither on the vine. You will know that there is a better way, but lack the influence and political skill to make it happen. More than likely, you will become increasingly cynical and resentful in response to the pull of the organization in directions favoring the current business and sustaining products. You will be unhappy.

Dream

Our dream for you, your potential customers, and your firm is that you will succeed, that you will take up the challenge of uncovering important customer problems, learning to navigate the organization even better than you do now, and bringing a stream of breakthrough products to market.

With great admiration and respect,
Abbie, Ray, and Bruce

Dear Aspiring Serial Innovators:

We've come to realize over the years we've been doing this research just how critical you may be to the competitive future of your organization, and perhaps even to your country. It is extremely difficult for a start-up company to invent and commercialize massively complex breakthrough products. Many of them need to be created in the context of a (large) mature firm. We need you to do it.

Hope
Our hope is that you will engage in serious self-assessment and that, as you reflect on your own skills and inclinations in light of those characteristics that we describe, you see what you need to do and have the determination to do it. Our hope, too, is that you have Serial Innovator role models and technical managers who can aid you in such development. Go seek them out.

Fear
Our first fear on your behalf is that you have not yet "crossed the bridge" by taking personal responsibility to see innovative insights all the way to market. Don't simply rely on "someone else" to recognize the value of your insights and carry them to completion on the organization's behalf. Our second fear for you, not unlike our fear for existing Serial Innovators, is that you may lose heart, commitment, or focus. Please do not. Your potential for impact is too great.

Challenge
Our first challenge is that you "cross the bridge" and, then, like current Serial Innovators, continue and persevere to invest yourself to understand deeply the subtleties of customer needs, and that you will continue to demonstrate courage in serving customer and company alike. Our second challenge is, if you find that you do not have the necessary temperament or capabilities to contribute as a Serial Innovator, that you support those who do, developing as a key contributor in another sig-

nificant innovation role, be that an Inventor, Champion, Implementer, or manager of Serial Innovators.

"Blessing"

If you rise to our two challenges, you will either succeed by discovering how to find and understand important problems and navigate your organization or will come to realize that certain factors are missing that cannot be overcome. Thus, you will either bring new insights to market or have the confidence to move on to more fruitful organizational grounds.

"Curse"

If you cannot rise to the challenge of "crossing the bridge," you will either wither on the vine, if your aspiration truly is to become a Serial Innovator, or you will come to understand that you really are not a potential Serial Innovator and you will move into a different role in the organization. Persevering as an aspiring Serial Innovator will only make you increasingly bitter and resentful at your inability to become one.

Dream

Our dream for you is that you will succeed, that you will accurately assess your skills and tendencies, and that you will move to a role where your strengths are valued and be very productive. If that role is to be a Serial Innovator, that means learning to understand customer needs deeply, finding important problems to solve, solving them, and navigating the organization to bring them to fruition.

With great hope for your future,
Abbie, Ray, and Bruce

Dear Serial Innovator Colleagues—Inventors, Champions, Implementers:

You are critically important to the firm for several reasons. First, you are crucial in helping the firm sustain and refresh its ongoing businesses through developing the new products on which you primarily work. Please remember that these efforts represent more than 75% of firms' NPD projects. Without you, the firm cannot remain in business. However, you also are critical in helping support Serial Innovators' efforts in moving into new white space. They will seek you out for your technical knowledge, your ability to lead, your peer networks, and your skill at making things happen.

Hope
We hope that this book has helped to clarify the various roles that are important for developing new products, and has shown you the value of your work. We also hope that this book has illuminated why Serial Innovators do things differently from the formal process in the organization. We hope your understanding of Serial Innovators will help you to support them in their efforts and to appreciate their differences.

Fear
One fear we have is that we have made you want to be something that just is not a fit for you, given your personality, perspective, and inherent motivations. Not everyone is meant to be a Serial Innovator.

Challenge
Our challenge to you is threefold. First, be the very best that you can be by continuously honing the skills needed to be most successful in your role in the firm. Second, learn to recognize and support the Serial Innovators in your organization and become comfortable with how their contributions differ from yours. Finally, if you review Chapter 1, you will see that the market and customer understanding tasks can be missing in the formal invention-championship-implementation model of NPD. Would some of you please take responsibility for overcoming these shortcomings of this process?

"Blessing"

We believe that if you are honest with yourself and rise to the challenges above, you will contribute both to sustaining the current business and growing the business into new white space. By being true to your personal strengths, you will be happiest. You will find that working with Serial Innovators on breakthrough innovations will be energizing.

"Curse"

Aspiring to be something that is not in your nature or capabilities will only make you unhappy. It likely also will lead to jealousy of those who can do what you cannot. These attitudes likely will ultimately be noticed by management, perhaps leading to marginalization in the organization.

Dream

Our dream for you is that you understand and believe how valuable you are to the organization, that you grow in your role to your fullest capability, and that you have the opportunity to help at least one Serial Innovator in their breakthrough innovation efforts.

With admiration and respect,
Abbie, Ray, and Bruce

Dear Students:

What is that old saying?—"The world is your oyster." And what this book should tell you is that "pearls" come in many colors, each of them beautiful.

Hope
Our hope is that you are intrigued by the idea of contributing to the success of your future organization. We also hope that you take this time as a student to reflect on your strengths, weaknesses, and underlying motivations, as well as to work on areas most in need of development, whether they be self-awareness, broad and deep insights, learning to learn, curiosity, or creativity. Explore what you could be. Think now about what role in the organization might best suit your personality, motivations, and innate skill sets, whether it be an Inventor, Champion, Implementer, Innovator, manager, entrepreneur, or ultimately some role outside of innovation and technology.

Fear
Perhaps our greatest fear is that you do not sufficiently or purposefully develop skills for your future. At the other end of the spectrum, we also are concerned that you not become inappropriately enamored with the role of a Serial Innovator. Although critical, the Serial Innovator is just one of many roles that contribute effectively to every organization. We fear, as one of our colleagues put it, that you not want to merely "be" a Serial Innovator, but, instead, that you come to know what it is that you want to "do." If what you want to do with your career—what motivates you at your core—is not consistent with the role of a Serial Innovator, by all means, we encourage you to pursue another path.

Challenge
Our challenge, then, is that you persevere in deeply understanding yourself, to prepare most effectively for the entirety of your career. At the same time, we expect and challenge you to develop yourself in areas of personal weakness that have been identified as characteristics of successful Serial Innovators in this book. Regardless of the role you play

in your future organization, whether in a large firm or an entrepreneurial start-up, many of the Serial Innovator skills as described herein will serve you well.

"Blessing"

If you rise to this expectation and challenge, you will succeed, because success is defined as doing what is the right fit for you—your personality, your perspectives, and your motivations. Even if you never contribute directly as a Serial Innovator, you will contribute in a way fitting for who you are.

"Curse"

If you do not rise to these personal challenges, you will fail. Failure here can mean many things, including attempting to be something that you are not, attempting to present yourself as something that you are not, or failing to develop skills that will serve you and your organization. You will be unhappy doing something for which you are not well suited.

Dream

Our dream is that you will find the right fit between who you are and the career options available to you. If that fit is for you to become a Serial Innovator, our dream is that we have encouraged and guided you along this difficult but fulfilling path.

With great hope for a bright and promising future,
Abbie, Ray, and Bruce

Dear Technical Managers:

Well, as should be absolutely crystal clear to you at this point: without you, there can be no Serial Innovators in an organization. Your personal relationship capabilities are virtually the only way that an aspiring Serial Innovator can become a Serial Innovator. You hold the future of the organization in your hands. We cannot emphasize this point strongly enough.

Hope
Our hope is that these stories have resonated with and encouraged you. We hope that you saw yourself in how you manage those who fit the Serial Innovator or potential Serial Innovator profile, and also those who serve in other roles, especially Inventors. We hope that you have had the privilege to serve your customers and organization by working insightfully and effectively with Serial Innovators. We also hope that this book will help provide the foundation you need to protect Serial Innovators from standardizing HR policies and impatient executives.

Fear
Still, we fear that you have Serial Innovators but don't deal effectively with them. Usually, this failure is characterized by not providing the resources, time, or access required by Serial Innovators to innovate. However, it also can occur by over- or undermanaging them or even by competing with them for visibility, financial reward, and promotions. Second, we fear that you might not take the time to develop those with the potential to become Serial Innovators by not giving them sufficiently challenging technical problems, appropriate exposure to customer needs, or freedom to explore innovative possibilities. We understand that you might be reluctant to do so because it takes so much time and because you, too, will have to become something of a renegade, and this is difficult in formalized organizational structures. Third, we fear that you might not deal effectively with those who are not Serial Innovators, perhaps by misidentifying potential Serial Innovators and giving people without the essential characteristics a license to indulge themselves—a mistake that will be recognized and resented by true Serial Innovators.

Finally, we fear that, in spite of your best effort, powers beyond your control will overrule your attempts to either develop or work effectively with such individuals as we have described herein.

Challenge

Our challenge, then, is that you reflect carefully on your personal situation, particularly seeking to understand deeply your own motivations and aspirations as well as the characteristics and personalities of those who report to you, including the subtleties of their strengths, weaknesses, and potentials for development. We encourage you to get to know those across your organization who have successfully filled the Serial Innovator role or managed Serial Innovators. Use the insights developed within those relationships to better understand how to effectively identify, develop, and manage those for whom you have organizational responsibility. Appropriately fight the political fight, build for the long term, and seek paradigm and structural shifts.

"Blessing"

In many respects, the expectations on the managers of Serial Innovators are as high or higher than those to which we hold Serial Innovators. However, if you rise to these challenges, you also will either succeed by discovering how to manage effectively in your organization or by realizing that certain factors are missing that cannot be overcome. Thus, you will either contribute appropriately to bringing new insights to market or will have the confidence to move on to more fruitful organizational grounds.

"Curse"

If you do not rise to these challenges, unlike the Serial Innovators, you may not wither on the vine. Instead, there is the likelihood that you might even be promoted to higher levels of responsibility within your organization, having not permitted failure by engaging in what might be labeled as "reckless" attempts to bring "risky" new ideas to the marketplace. However, those who see and understand will know the truth, and your ability to lead at these higher levels will be compromised, undermined by your having taken a self-serving path at this stage in your career.

Dream

Our dream for you, your Serial Innovators, your potential customers, and your firm is that you will succeed. We hope you will take up the challenge of learning to successfully identify, develop, and support not only the Serial Innovators in your organization, but those fulfilling all of the roles critical to innovation.

With great respect,
Abbie, Ray, and Bruce

Dear Human Resource Managers:

Unfortunately, Serial Innovators are round pegs to the square holes of a large, mature organization's equalizing human resource policies. They and their managers have the potential to be the bane of your existence.

Hope

Our hope is that this book helps you to recognize your organization's Serial Innovators and the insightful technical managers who know how to navigate your organization effectively and to realize just how crucial they are to the long-term success of the firm. We also hope that you can use this material to learn how to effectively operate as a human resource manager both with exemplar individuals such as Serial Innovators and with the rest of your organization.

Fear

Our fears are twofold. First, we are concerned that your firm's HR function will operate too strictly within organizational policies that are geared toward the typical employee when some circumstances and individuals simply beg for some appropriate "breaking" of the rules. Second, we fear that your HR function has not appropriately gauged the impact of how you reward those whose contributions are questionable at best, so that in spite of your best efforts to motivate the organization, the net result is a lessening of impact.

Challenge

Our challenge, then, is that you reflect carefully on your personal situation, particularly seeking to understand deeply the strengths and the limitations of the organization's current HR policies. Not unlike the expectations we placed on the technical managers, we encourage you, too, to get to know those across your organization who have successfully filled the Serial Innovator role, and those who have identified, developed, and managed them, with the goal of using the insights developed within those relationships to better understand how to effectively support those for whom you have organizational responsibility. We also challenge you to figure out how to construct interview protocols that will help your organization identify potential Serial Innovators at the entry level.

"Blessing"

If you rise to these challenges, you will contribute in ways beyond those in which most HR managers can or will. Thus, you will have helped to bring new insights to market, impacting your organization's bottom line and long-term survival.

"Curse"

If you do not rise to the challenge, you will join the ranks of those unfortunates labeled as "Catbert-like"! You will have succeeded in implementing efficient, standardized, equalizing organizational policies while impeding Serial Innovators' from developing groundbreaking products. Although these hindrances may be unlikely to impact your career adversely, they will harm the firm in the long term.

Dream

Our dream is that you have gained insight into how to identify and develop Serial Innovators. Further, we hope that you will value them, in spite of their being outliers who may require additional personal investment on your part in the short term. Our dream is that you will take on the challenges identified above and succeed, learning to discern and respond to the needs of these key contributors in your organization in new, creative—even innovative—ways with insight and wisdom. In many respects, you, too, may be called on to be a renegade in your organization, something not typically in the job description of an HR manager. In total, our dream is that you will build an HR capability for supporting a personal model of breakthrough innovation in your organization.

With encouragement and anticipation of great outcomes,
Abbie, Ray, and Bruce

Dear Senior Technical Executive (CTO):

One of your tasks is to create the innovation space in your organization where Serial Innovators can exist and where they are encouraged and supported. Creating this space means making the appropriate long-term investments and engaging personally with Serial Innovators. If you do not know who the Serial Innovators are in your organization, shame on you! Worse, if there are none . . . well, you have failed your organization.

Hope

Our hope is that this resonated with you, and that, because of this book, you now realize that your organization has both Serial Innovators and insightful technical managers. We hope you know each of them personally and that they know you are a supporter and Champion. We hope, as well, that you already take a longer-term view, understanding that Serial Innovators help you build an organization that is capable of true innovation.

Fear

Having said this, perhaps our worst fear is that you have risen through your organization by ignoring the important roles played by such individuals, and that you have "succeeded" by succumbing to the pressures of the rest of the organization, by taking the less difficult, incremental innovation path without planting the seeds of long-term, sustainable organizational success. Our second fear is that you will not have the courage to help your technical managers identify, develop, and support Serial Innovators and potential Serial Innovators—that you will continue to take the path of least resistance.

Challenge

Our challenge, then, is that you invest in those who can contribute in such exemplary ways and in the managers who can manage them effectively. We encourage you to support both Serial Innovators and their technical managers with resources, organizational policy latitude, and organizational space appropriate to the innovation task at hand. We challenge you to invest in developing Serial Innovators and managers alike, fostering their growth in ways that positively impact the firm's future.

"Blessing"

If you rise to this expectation and challenge, you will benefit all involved. You will have enabled Serial Innovators to bring new breakthrough products to market. You also will have significantly served your organization's customers and shareholders. Further, you will have rightfully earned the respect of your organization for having facilitated "the greater good."

"Curse"

If you do not rise to the challenge, you will very likely survive comfortably, as will your organization for some time. However, eventually your organization will no longer be able to sustain and grow; it will have thrived in the short term only to wither or die in the long term. Your organization will have lost its ability to remake itself and this will have occurred on your watch, even though it likely will become evident only after you retire or move on. Those who remember you will appropriately question your judgment and willingness to take on appropriate risk in advocating for organizational renewal.

Dream

Our dream for you, your potential customers, and your organization is that you will succeed—that you will take up these challenges, learning to lead your technical organization with impact and with managerial sensitivity for the needs of (and for) individuals who fulfill each of the various roles in innovation.

With respect,
Abbie, Ray, and Bruce

Dear Senior Business Executive (CEO or President):

You are critical because you set the tone for what is important in your organization. You determine if the organization will focus on growth over the long term or if you will only focus on short-term, quarterly performance. Your perspectives will determine if Serial Innovators will find a welcome home in your organization.

Hope

Our hope is that this encouraged you, and that you saw yourself and your organization as it seeks to address customer needs and shareholder expectations. We hope that you now believe that breakthrough innovation can occur in your large, mature firm, rather than just in start-up firms, as others previously have suggested. Our desire is that you realize the critically important role of Serial Innovators and their technical managers in your organization—roles that are at the foundation of whether your organization will survive well beyond your watch. We hope that you take a long-term view of strategic growth and not simply cut costs when confronted with financial challenges.

Fear

Our fear is that you may be pulled too easily into the tyranny of the business sustainment needs of the moment. We fear that you will redirect resources away from what is needed to move into new organizational white spaces or that you will not be sufficiently patient to see those new product categories grow and mature. We also fear that your organization's hiring practices, although well intended, may actually be winnowing out those with the inherent skills to become Serial Innovators. Finally, we fear that there may be no way for your organization to acquire deep, significant customer insight that makes market-driven breakthrough innovation possible.

Challenge

Our expectation and challenge, then, is that you take the messages contained herein to heart. We challenge you to invest yourself to understand deeply what exists and what is missing in your organization. We challenge you to seek the counsel and guidance of those with proven track records as Serial Innovators and those who have successfully managed them. We encourage you to develop sufficient judgment and discernment in these areas to make the difficult decisions necessary to continue to bring new breakthrough innovations to market while simultaneously operating efficient, sustainable ongoing current business operations. We challenge you to build a true organizational capability to innovate by investing in a portfolio that encourages new product categories and renewal.

"Blessing"

If you rise to these expectations and challenges, you will have served all. You will have played a key role in bringing important new products to customers. You will have fulfilled the most challenging investor expectations, both near term and long term. You will have provided the environment in which others may succeed and experience fulfilling careers. You will be known and remembered as being a wise and efficient steward of what has been entrusted to you.

"Curse"

If you do not rise to the challenge, you will very likely survive comfortably, as will your organization for some time. However, eventually your organization will no longer be able to survive, sustain, and grow. It will have lost its ability to remake itself and this will have occurred on your watch, even though it likely will become evident only after you have retired or moved on. Most such organizations die or, at best, are acquired. Those individuals who remember you will question your judgment and willingness to take on appropriate risk in advocating for organizational renewal.

Dream

Our dream is that you will succeed, and that you will take up the challenge, learning to lead your organization in a manner not often witnessed.

With hope for you and your organization's future,
Abbie, Ray, and Bruce

Interview Suggestions for Identifying
Potential Serial Innovators

Most of the suggestions that follow are simple questions and situations that might be employed in a typical formal interview or informal conversation in search of those with potential for breakthrough innovation. With some modification, these questions can be used at any career stage or experience level.

PERSONALITY CHARACTERISTICS THAT
SUPPORT CREATION: CURIOSITY, INTUITION,
CREATIVITY, AND SYSTEMS THINKING

- Give the candidate a basket of "gadgets" to choose from. Let him or her select one of the items and then give the candidate two minutes to present what it is and how it works. This exercise assesses curiosity: can they find something they know about given a range of gadgets, and do they understand how each really works?

- In conversation, look for wide-ranging interests such as "seeking as much information as I can in a new situation," "looking for new opportunities to grow as a person," or "looking for new things and experiences everywhere I go." Also look for multiple hobbies and avocations.

- In conversation, look for the tendency to dive deeply into a topic or area of interest.

- Present candidates with a unique situation and observe how many ideas they can create in one to two minutes. Then have them describe in more detail each of the options.

- Seek examples where the candidate has looked at the same data as others, but in a different light. Consider how the candidate integrates or reframes ideas.

- When the candidate describes his or her work, does he or she tend to focus on the boundaries and the interfaces with other systems? Does he or she describe the parts and discuss how each part is optimized, or describe how to optimize the entire system—even if some elements are suboptimized?

- Have candidates describe times when they have trusted their intuition concerning their technical work. What did they do and what happened?

- Do they understand why things work the way they do? Have them describe any system they are working with, and have them explain why it works the way it does.

PERSONALITY CHARACTERISTICS THAT SUPPORT INNOVATION: INDEPENDENCE, CONFIDENCE, TAKING CALCULATED RISKS, AND PERSEVERANCE

- Have candidates describe their biggest challenges or most difficult problems. Did they consciously choose the more difficult problems or were they frustrated to find themselves working on a problem that was harder than anticipated?

- What projects have they brought to fruition? What have they completed? What difference did it make?

- If you said it would take us five to ten years or more to bring something to the market, how would the candidates approach that type of problem? Would they want to work on it? What would they do? Is there any evidence that they can keep their motivation and focus over an extended period of time?

- Look for evidence that they have mastered some difficult activity that took many years. Hobbies such as music performance, art, competitive sports, or martial arts might demonstrate this persistence effectively.

- Do they exhibit the confidence to share their creative ideas with others? If there was push back, what happened? Did they endure? Did they refine, improve, and come back? What have they learned on their own, just because they wanted to learn it? There should be several examples of both large and small tasks that they have taken on independently. They may have risked a grade or class standing for their independent understanding.

PERSPECTIVES ON BUSINESS

- Why does a company exist?
- What are your company's revenues and what percent profit does your company make?
- Is your company's profit too much or too little? Why?
- What financial performance does your company exhibit relative to its competition?
- How do research and development (R&D) and new product development (NPD) add to shareholder value?
- Would they rather work on a new breakthrough technology or a new breakthrough product? Why?
- Ask them if they could bring a new product to market with off-the-shelf technology versus newly developed technology, which project would they work on? Why?
- Have candidates tell you about any jobs they had where they had to work directly with a customer. What did they like? What didn't they like?
- Have the candidate discuss how they might go about understanding a customer. How would they understand a product or service from the customer's perspective?

PERSPECTIVES ON PEOPLE

- If your team needed a skill that you didn't have, what would you do?
- If your team needed a skill that you didn't have, assuming you would add someone with that skill, how would you go about recruiting that person to join your team?
- Describe how you have influenced other people—individuals, small groups, and large groups—in both the short term and in the long term.
- Tell us what type of people would want to work with you. Why?
- Tell us about the people in your life whom you have really valued. How did you communicate/demonstrate that to them?

PERSPECTIVES ON PERSONAL RESPONSIBILITY AND HARD WORK

- What would the candidate like to work hard to change about the world in his or her lifetime?
- Is there evidence that the interviewee works hard and takes personal responsibility for everything he or she does?
- When the interviewee talks about projects, is it clear that he or she has taken initiative and assumed responsibility?
- When asked about their failures, does the interviewee take personal responsibility or is there a tendency to blame others or situational factors?
- To what does the interviewee attribute their success?

MOTIVATION: CHALLENGES, JOY OF DISCOVERY, PROFOUND UNDERSTANDING, AND ACHIEVING RESULTS

- Does the interviewee really understand the fundamentals of his or her discipline?
- When you discuss any of the interviewee's major projects, does he or she demonstrate profound understanding and insights?
- When candidates describe problems that they have engaged with, do they speak with passion and spark, or with detached rationality?

- Have the candidates describe how they work on a problem that they want to solve. Do they think about it all the time—eat, drink, and sleep the problem?

- Has the interviewee demonstrated completing projects and accomplishing results? Or has he or she been content with completing the assigned tasks?

SUMMARY

We have found that the personality characteristics associated with creating (curiosity and systems thinking) are the primary characteristics related to how Serial Innovators engage with problems. Serial Innovators' methods for undertaking projects are affected by their personality characteristics that support innovation—primarily persistence—and their perspectives on working hard and taking personal responsibility. Their perspectives on business and on people influence the type of projects they select and how they are able to execute those projects by getting the right people on board. Finally, Serial Innovators' intrinsic motivation to solve customer problems and their desire for profound understanding and for finding great joy in discovery enables them to find, understand, and solve important customer problems.

REFERENCES

Allen, Thomas J. 1966. "Studies of the Problem-Solving Process in Engineering Design." *IEEE Transactions on Engineering Management* 13 (2): 72–83.

Amabile, Teresa M. 1988. "A Model of Creativity and Innovation in Organizations." *Research in Organizational Behavior* 10:123–67.

Barczak Gloria, Abbie Griffin, and Kenneth B. Kahn. 2009. "PERSPECTIVE: Trends and Drivers of Success in NPD Practices: Results of the 2003 PDMA Best Practices Study." *Journal of Product Innovation Management* 25 (January): 3–23.

Barton, Allen W. 2009. "Opening the Box on Serial Innovators: Exploring the Personality, Motivation, and Perspective of Elite Individuals Involved in New Product Development." MS thesis, University of Illinois at Urbana-Champaign.

Brunner, G. F. 2001. "The IRI Medalist's Address: The Tao of Innovation." *Research-Technology Management* 44 (1): 45–51.

Christensen, Clayton M. 1997. *The Innovator's Dilemma: When New Technologies Cause Great Firms to Fail.* Cambridge, MA: Harvard Business School Press.

Cooper, Robert G. 1996. *Winning at New Products.* Reading, MA: Addison-Wesley Publishing Company.

De Bono, Edward. 1973. *Lateral Thinking: Creativity Step by Step.* New York: Harper Colophon.

Deci, Edward L., and Richard M. Ryan. 1985. *Intrinsic Motivation and Self-Determination in Human Behavior (Perspectives in Social Psychology).* New York: Plenum Press.

Griffin, Abbie, Raymond L. Price, Matthew M. Maloney, Bruce Vojak, and Edward W. Sim. 2009. "Voices from the Field: How Exceptional Electronic Industrial Innovators Innovate." *Journal of Product Innovation Management* 26 (2): 222–40.

Griffin, Abbie, Edward W. Sim, Ray Price, and Bruce Vojak. 2007. "Exploring Differences Between Inventors, Champions, Implementers and Serial Innovators in Developing New Products in Large, Mature Firms." *Creativity and Innovation Management* 16 (4): 422–36.

Hebda, John M., Abbie Griffin, Bruce A. Vojak, and Raymond L. Price. 2007. "The Motivation of Technical Visionaries in Large American Companies." *IEEE Transactions on Engineering Management* 54 (3): 433–44.

———. 2012. "Motivating and Demotivating Technical Visionaries in Large Corporations: A Comparison of Perspectives." *R&D Management.*

Hiebert, Paul G. 2008. *Transforming Worldviews: An Anthropological Understanding of How People Change.* Grand Rapids, MI: Baker Academic.

House, Charles H. 2011. *Permission Denied: Odyssey of an Intrapreneur from "The Medal of Defiance" to the Corporate Boardroom.* Manuscript in preparation.

House, Charles, and Raymond Price. 2009. *The HP Phenomenon: Innovation and Business Transformation.* Palo Alto, CA: Stanford University Press.

Kashdan, Todd B., Paul Rose, and Frank D. Fincham. 2004. "Curiosity and Exploration: Facilitating Positive Subjective Experiences and Personal Growth Opportunities." *Journal of Personality Assessment* 82:291–305.

Kelley, Tom, with Jonathan Littman. 2000. *The Art of Innovation: Success Through Innovation the IDEO Way.* New York: Currency.

Koen, Peter A., Greg M. Ajamian, Scott Boyce, Allen Clamen, Eden Fisher, Stavros Fountoulakis, Albert Johnson, Pushpinder Puri, and Rebecca Seibert. 2002. "Fuzzy Front End: Effective Methods, Tools, and Techniques." In *The PDMA ToolBook for New Product Development*, edited by Paul Belliveau, Abbie Griffin, and Stephen Somermeyer, 5–36. New York: John Wiley & Sons.

Kuehl, Robert O. 1999. *Design of Experiments: Statistical Principles of Research Design and Analysis.* North Scituate, MA: Duxbury Press.

Liefer, Richard, Christopher M. McDermott, Gina Colarelli O'Connor, Lois S. Peters, Mark Rice, and Robert W. Veryzer. 2000. *Radical Innovation: How*

Mature Companies Can Outsmart Upstarts. Boston, MA: Harvard Business School Press.

Lightman, Sam. 1992. "The Eight-Year Overnight Success Story." *HP Measure* (November–December): 8–10.

Lovelace, R. F. 1986. "Stimulating Creativity Through Managerial Intervention." *R&D Management* 16:161–74.

Macaulay, Linda, Claire Moxham, Barbara Jones, and Ian Miles. 2010. "Innovation and Skills: Future Service Science Education." In *Handbooks of Service Science*, edited by Paul P. Maglio, Cheryl A. Kieliszewski, and James C. Spohrer, 717–36. London: Springer Science+Business Media.

Maidique, Modesto A. 1980. "Entrepreneurs, Champions, and Technological Innovation." *Sloan Management Review* 58 (6): 59–76.

Markham, Stephen K. 2002. "Product Champions: Crossing the Valley of Death." In *The PDMA ToolBook for New Product Development*, edited by Paul Belliveau, Abbie Griffin, and Stephen Somermeyer, 119–40. New York: John Wiley & Sons.

Markham, Stephen K., and Lynda Aimon-Smith. 2001. "Product Champions: Truth, Myths and Management." *Research-Technology Management* 44 (3): 44–51.

Meek, Esther. 2003. *Longing to Know.* Ada, MI: Brazos Press.

Miles, I., and B. Jones. 2008. "Innovation in the European Service Economy— Scenarios and Implications for Skills and Knowledge." European Techno-Economic Policy Support Network. http://eteps.gopa-cartermill.com/?p=248.

Narver, John C., and Stanley F. Slater. 1990. "The Effect of a Marketing Orientation on Business Profitability." *Journal of Marketing Research* 54 (4): 20–35.

Naugle, David K. 2002. *Worldview: The History of a Concept.* Grand Rapids, MI: William B. Eerdmans Publishing Company.

N. E. Thing Enterprises, eds. 1993. *Magic Eye: A New Way of Looking at the World.* Kansas City, MO: Andrews and McMeel Publishing.

Nicholson, G. C. 1998. "Keeping Innovation Alive." *Research-Technology Management* 41 (3): 34–40.

O'Brien, Jeffrey M. 2009. "IBM's Grand Plan to Save the Planet." *Fortune Magazine*, May 4, 84–91. http://money.cnn.com/2009/04/20/technology/obrien_ibm.fortune/index.htm.

O'Connor, Gina C., Richard Leifer, Albert S. Paulson, and Lois S. Peters. 2008. *Grabbing Lightning.* San Francisco, CA: Jossey-Bass.

Pink, Daniel H. 2009. *Drive: The Surprising Truth About What Motivates Us.* New York: Riverhead Books.

Polanyi, Michael. 1966. *The Tacit Dimension.* London: Routledge Press.

Price, Raymond L., Abbie Griffin, Bruce A. Vojak, Nathan Hoffman, and Holli Burgon. 2009. "Innovation Politics: How Serial Innovators Gain Organizational Acceptance for Breakthrough New Products." *International Journal of Technology Marketing* 4 (2–3): 165–84.

Rice, Mark, Donna Kelley, Lois Peters, and Gina Colarelli O'Connor. 2001. "Radical Innovation: Triggering Initiation of Opportunity Recognition and Evaluation." *R&D Management* 31 (4): 409–31.

Sarasvathy, Saras. 2001. "Causation and Effectuation: Toward a Theoretical Shift from Economic Inevitability to Entrepreneurial Contingency." *Academy of Management Review* 26 (2): 243–63.

Schumpeter, Joseph A. 1934. *The Theory of Economic Development.* Cambridge, MA: Harvard University Press.

Smith, Preston G., and Donald G. Reinertsen. 1992. "Shortening the Product Development Cycle Source." *Research-Technology Management* 35 (3): 44–49.

Sternberg, Robert J. 2007. *Wisdom, Intelligence and Creativity Synthesized.* Cambridge: Cambridge University Press.

Termin, L. 2002. "Nurturing Innovation." Presentation given at IEEE International Engineering Management Conference, Cambridge, UK, August 18–20.

Thompson, Paul H., Gene W. Dalton, and Richard Kopelman. 1974. "But What Have You Done for Me Lately?—The Boss." *IEEE Spectrum* 12 (10): 85–89.

Treffinger, Donald, Scott Isaksen, and Brian Stead-Doval. 2006. *Creative Problem-Solving: An Introduction, Fourth Edition.* Austin, TX: Prufrock Press.

Vojak, Bruce, Abbie Griffin, Raymond L. Price, and Konstantin Perlov. 2006. "Characteristics of Technical Visionaries as Perceived by American and British Industrial Physicists." *R&D Management* 36 (1): 17–24.

Vojak, Bruce, Raymond L. Price, and Abbie Griffin. 2010. "Corporate Innovation." In *The Oxford Handbook of Interdisciplinarity*, edited by Robert Frodeman, Julie Thompson Klein, and Carl Mitcham, 546–59. Oxford: Oxford University Press.

Williams, Sandra L. 2001. "The Relationship Between Shared Work Values and Interpersonal Trust Among Individuals in Selected Work Settings." PhD dissertation, University of Illinois at Urbana-Champaign.

Italic page numbers indicate material in tables or figures. The letter "n" after a page number signifies a reference to a footnote on that page.

acceleration phase, 27, 62n
aggregate market information, 77–78
"Aha!" moments, 52, 96. *See also* discernment/intuition
air pollution, 78–79, 106
airports, remote machine-built, 44–45, 105
Al (medical devices manager), 165
Alberto Culver, 1, 183
Always® Ultra feminine hygiene pad, 3–9, 83, 85, 90
ambiguity, tolerance for, 42
analogous domains, drawing from, 56–57, 61
Andersh, Dennis (Serial Innovator manager, SAIC), 154–59, 168–69
antiaging ointment, 84–85
apprenticeship with other Serial Innovators, 144
auto industry, 15–16
autonomy, 127
awards, 167

awareness, focal and subsidiary, 82

backwards, working, 44–45
ballroom dancing, managing as, 164–65
Bernick, Carol (Serial Innovator, Alberto Culver), 1–2
bias, 76
Biomax® (DuPont), 20–21
birds, letting them fly, 152, 162, 177
bobbers, 60, 120
breadth and depth of interests, 116–17, 130
breaking the rules, 110
breakthrough innovation: creating, 18–22; defined, 15; innovator-driven, 27–29, 35; market-driven, 22; in mature firms, 14; organizational resistance to, 89–91; predicting demand for, 80; risks of, 17–18; technology-push-driven, 19–21
buy-in, getting, 100–103

calculated risks, 111, 121, 204–5
car industry, U.S., 15–16
Carlton Society (3M), 173
Catbert, 154, 198
Caterpillar, 44, 57, 98, 183
challenge, need for, 206–7
Champions/sponsors, 23–27; for
    Always Ultra concept, 8; enlist-
    ing help from, 102, 142; Inventor-
    Champion-Implementer scenario,
    177–79; love letter to, 190–91;
    mentoring by, 142; and Valley of
    Death, 27, 94
Christensen, Clayton M., 113,
    168–69
circular processes, 19, 37, 51, 59, 69
coach role, 32, 130, 132, 142
commercialization, seeing through
    to, 128–29, 160–61
common good as value, 114, 124–25
competence builds trust, 91–94
competition, understanding the, 47,
    51, 79, 142
concern for others, 93
conferences, 79–80
confidence, 114, 121, 138–39, 204–5
conjoint analysis, 84
connections: between dots, 49, 51,
    60, 119–20, 127; predisposition to
    expect, 135
consensus is not truth, 81
constraints, 55
convergence of technology, customer
    needs, market, 28, 32–33
cooking oil, 49, 55–56, 66, 85, 104
coworkers, caring about, 125–26
creativity, 61, 114, 118, 136, 203–4
credibility, 80
credit, giving and sharing, 93
cross-function fertilization, 156
crossing the bridge of political real-
    ity, 94–99, 108, 142, 145
cross terms, 61

curiosity, 114–18, 120, 127–28, 131,
    203–4
customers: deep knowledge of, 42,
    46; defined, 70n; of difference, 72,
    81; engagement at end of develop-
    ment, 128–29; engagement during
    development, 83–84; enlisting to
    influence organizational decisions,
    108, 162–63; focus on individual,
    72–77; going to their location, 75;
    identifying right, 73–74; immer-
    sion, 50–51, 71, 73–74, 87, 159;
    importance of early exposure to,
    142–43; managers as internal,
    108–9; perspective of, 47; retain-
    ing over time, 15; using models to
    connect with, 59, 106–7
cynicism, avoiding, 97

data quality and validity, 80–81
Dave (nut roasting Innovator), 50,
    58, 92, 117–18
daydreaming, 118
Defense Electromagnetics Company
    (DEMACO), 154–56
demonstrations, 59, 106–7
depth and breadth of interests, 116–
    17, 130
diagnostic information, 84
diaper industry, 56–57, 86
Dilbert, 154
directed motivation, 32
discernment/intuition, 52, 60, 118; as
    identifying characteristic of Serial In-
    novators, 136, 203–4; and indwell-
    ing, 81–82; and influencing others,
    96, 108–9. See also connections
discovery, joy of, 127–28
discovery phase, 27
do-it-yourself (DIY) mentality, 86
dots: finding then connecting, 49, 51,
    60, 119–20, 127, 138; stereogram
    images, 82

drive for profound understanding, 128–29, 131
drug-eluting stents, 56, 91
DuPont Biomax®, 20–21
dust balls, groups of knowledge as, 60, 119–20
dynamic Ts, 130–31

early career actions of Serial Innovators, 91–99, 103, 141–43
Eberhard, Martin (Serial Innovator, NuvoMedia, Tesla Motors), 2
Edison, Thomas, 41
education and training: business courses, 143; formal, 129–31; on-the-job learning, 130–31, 144; self-directed, 116, 144–45
Electronic Design Magazine, 1–2, 12
electronic device Innovator, 108
emphysema and air pollution, 78–79, 106, 128
engaging with people, 100–103, 139–40
engaging with projects, 137–39
engaging with the business, 139
Engineering Hall of Fame, 12
engineers: interactions with customers, 71–75, 88; managing, 88, 181; as team members, 97, 100; and technical model of feminine hygiene, 4, 119
ethics, 31
execution, 22–23, 62–65, *133*

face-to-face interactions, 64, 76, 101, 104
fail early and cheaply, 57
far-in-the-future visions, 44–45
fat-free butter flavoring, 1
Fellow positions, *169–70, 173–76*
feminine hygiene pads, 3–9, 44, 119
fertilization rate, 44–45

FFE. *See* Fuzzy Front End (FFE) of innovation
first of a kind (FOAK) projects, 20
first order effects, 71
"floating bobbers," 60, 120
FOAK, 20
focal awareness, 82
formal management policies, 153–54
formal product development processes, 16–18, 53, 62
Frank (heavy equipment Innovator), 64, 101–2
Fred (medical device Innovator), 45, 75, 165–66
freedom to explore, 92
"Fruitful System" companies, 147, 148–49
fundamental principles, 49–50, 55
"fuzzy dust balls," 60, 119–20
Fuzzy Front End (FFE) of innovation, 18–19; leading to proposed solution, 61–62; marketing not involved in, 24; Serial Innovators' process, 37–38; significant effort for breakthrough innovation, 18; too nonlinear to be a process, 19

Galileo scenario, 90
global optima, 58, 120, 128
GPS navigation, 44–45, 105
greater good as value, 114, 124–25
Gudat, Adam (Serial Innovator, Caterpillar), 44–45; finding analogous tasks, 57; incremental progress toward ultimate goal, 105; insistence on face-to-face contact, 64; involving engineers, 100; on leader role, 65; selling ideas to managers, 98; simulation software, 58–59
Gunsalus, C. K., 105

Hall, Jim (Serial Innovator, Hewlett-Packard), 122

hammers looking for nails, 20, 25

handcuffs, taking off, 158

hard influencing, 99, 106–8

heavy equipment team quilting exercise, 64, 101–2

Hewlett-Packard (HP), 1, 18, 122, 183–84; Hall, Jim, 122; Hewlett, Bill, 116, 181; House, Charles H. "Chuck," 1–2, 66, 78–79, 106, 111, 128, 182n

hiring challenges, 149–51

honesty, 93

hourglass model, 37–38, 84, 177

House, Charles H. "Chuck" (Serial Innovator, Hewlett-Packard), 1–2, 66, 78–79, 106, 111, 128, 182n

human resources, 149, 154, 160–68, 197–98

hunches, 52, 60, 118; as identifying characteristic of Serial Innovators, 136, 203–4; and indwelling, 81–82; and influencing others, 96, 108–9. See also connections

hypotheses, testing of, 58

IBM, 20, 173

idealism, 31, 35, 161, 167

identifying potential Serial Innovators, 135–40, 145–46

imaginary work, 159

Implementer role, 23–27, 129–30, 142, 177–78, 190

incremental innovation, 15, 18, 147

incubation phase, 27, 62n

incubator groups, 156–59, 169–72, 176

independence, 114, 120–21, 138–39, 204–5

Industrial Research Institute, 19

indwelling, 82

influencing: acceptance during the project, 34, 99–109; decisionmakers and team members, 98–109; flexible application of, 108–9; hard

tactics, 99, 106–8; soft tactics, 99, 104–6; supervisors, 95

information seeking, 115–16. See also multiple knowledge domains

infrastructure changes, 90–91

innovation: incremental and breakthrough, 15; processes, 161; roles and tasks involved in, 22–23; to support ongoing business, 15–17

innovator-driven breakthrough innovation, 27–29, 35

Innovator role, 25–27

integrating process and characteristics, 133

interesting problems, 39, 41, 45–46, 61–62, 144

internal customers, 70n, 108–9

interviewing potential Serial Innovators, 203–7

intrinsic desire, 32

intrinsic motivation, 115, 126–27, 136, 138, 146

intrinsic technical capabilities, 55

intuition, 52, 60, 118; as identifying characteristic of Serial Innovators, 136, 203–4; and indwelling, 81–82; and influencing others, 96, 108–9. See also connections

inventing and validating phase, 52–54, 133

Inventor role, 23–25, 27; distinguishing from Serial Innovator, 50, 136, 142, 145, 148, 150, 178–79; education and training, 129; ignorance/avoidance of organizational politics, 91, 94, 97, 103, 139; Inventor-Champion-Implementer scenario, 177–79; lack of interest in customer/market, 123, 139; love letter to, 190–91

iterating, 109

Jim (LCD lighting Innovator), 42–43, 51, 73–74

Jobs, Steve, 2
joy of discovery, 127–29, 131, 206–7
j work, 159

knowing, sense of, 52, 60, 118; as
    identifying characteristic of Se-
    rial Innovators, 136, 203–4; and
    indwelling, 81–82; and influenc-
    ing others, 96, 108–9. *See also*
    connections
"know-what" and "know-how," 150

laser-jet printers, 122
launch, 67
LCD lightbulb performance, 42–43,
    51, 73–74
leadership responsibility, 101
learning, desire for, 32, 127–28. *See
    also* education and training
learning plans, 47–48
Lee, Shung Wu "Andy" (Serial Inno-
    vator, DEMACO, SAIC), 154–59
liaison positions, 169–73, 175–76
lifelong learners, 32
listening effectively, 76–77
living the problem, 47
local optima, 58, 120
logic analyzer, 1, 18
"Losing the Formula" companies, 147
"lot in life" mentality, 126
love letters: to Aspiring Serial In-
    novators, 188–89; to Human
    Resource Managers, 197–98; to
    Inventors, Champions, Implement-
    ers, 190–91; products as, 50, 183n;
    to Senior Business Executive (CEO/
    President), 201–2; to Senior Tech-
    nical Executive (CTO), 199–200;
    to Serial Innovators, 186–87; to
    Students, 192–93; to Technical
    Managers, 194–96

Magic Eyes books, 82
managerial thinking, 178

managing Serial Innovators, 3, 30;
    barriers to overcome in, 179–82;
    concern about special treatment,
    177–79; in early career, 141–43,
    176; errors in, 166, 181; formal
    management practices, 166–68;
    handling time management, 40, 87,
    158–59, 161–62; individualized,
    informal management practices,
    160–66, 175; keeping projects "off
    the books," 162; in large, mature
    firms, 152–54; in late career, 146–
    47, 156–58; like ballroom dancing,
    164–65; managing engineers, 88;
    managing the pipeline, 147–49;
    multiple engagement methods, 181;
    potential Serial Innovators, 140–
    47; providing customer immersion
    opportunities, 143, 144, 159, 163;
    providing education opportunities,
    132; providing freedom, 146, 158–
    59; providing organizational space,
    168–76; providing resources, 163–
    64; showing willingness to learn,
    180–81; supporting risk-taking,
    181–82. *See also* identifying poten-
    tial Serial Innovators
Mark (food oil Innovator), 49, 55–
    56, 66, 85, 104
marketing: creating acceptance,
    65–67, 84–86, 133; market-pull
    initiatives, 27–28, 69; R&D liaison
    positions, 169–73, 175–76; re-
    search, 47, 51, 73, 75
mass recruiting policies, 150
mastery, 127–28
McCartney, Paul, 2
"Medal of Defiance," 9, 111
medical devices, 45, 75, 165–66
mentor/coach role, 32, 130, 132,
    142
models, 49–50, 57–59, 106–7
Molly McButter, 1
money/profit incentive, 115, 124–25

motivation, 30, 31, 114–15, 126–29, *133*, 206–7

MP⁵ model, 29–34, 114–16

Mrs. Dash, 1, 18

multiple approaches and solutions, 42–43, 46, 54–57

multiple engagement management, 181

multiple knowledge domains: curiosity across, 136, 138; education in, 32, 130–31; holistic exploration of problems, 48–49; peripheral fields of technology, 32, 42, 45; "π-shaped people," 130–31; "T-shaped people," 130; to understand marketplace, 77; visiting universities and incubators, 45; wide and deep exploration of, 138; within firm, 144

naïveté, 94, 96

nature, constraints of, 55

nature *versus* nurture, 116

needs understanding, 22–23, 25–28

networking, 91–94, 100, 106

new product development (NPD) processes: classical view of, 23; Serial Innovators' process, 9; transition from art to science, 36

new-to-the-world concepts, 17

next step forward, 44–45, 98

nonlinear process, 33, 39–40

nut roasting, 50, 58, 92, 117–18

NuvoMedia, 2

observation, 74–75

ointment, cream or lotion, 84–85

Oliver, Barney, 113

"One Hit Wonder" companies, *147*, 148

on-the-job learning, 130–31, 144

openness, 93

opportunity articulation, 52

organizational politics: choices for Serial Innovators, *170*, 175–76; crossing the bridge, 94–99, 108, 142, 145; influencing acceptance during the project, 34, 62, 99–109; organizational availability, 161; playing for high stakes and, 109–11; seen as "block of granite," 122

organizations, large and mature, 29–34

Osborn, Tom (Serial Innovator, Proctor & Gamble): Always® Ultra feminine hygiene pad, 3–9, 44; Champion support, 8, 90; cross terms in problem-solving, 61; indwelling, 82–83; involving coworkers, 100–101; and organizational politics, 96; persistence of, 109; products as love letters, 50; prototypes and product demonstrations, 85, 101, 107; qualitative modeling, 57; reframing the problem, 119; risk of termination, 6–7, 110–11; values making difference for customers, 124

π-shaped people, 130–31

Palm PDAs, 16

PalmPilot®, 17–18

paradigm changes, 182

paragraphs, hearing, 77

participation, getting volunteer, 100–103

patent awards, 123, 167–68

patent research, 45, 80

path toward innovation, 47, 52

periodicals, reading, 79

perseverance, 114, 121–22, 204–5

persistence, 109

personal interaction with customers, 50–51, 71–77, 87, 142–43, 159

personality: characteristics supporting creation, 203–4; characteristics supporting innovation, 204–5; characteristics supporting problem finding and understanding, 116–20, *133*; characteristics supporting project completion, 120–22; combined with perspective, motivation, 30–31, 114–15; immutability of, 115

perspective: on business, 205; combined with personality, motivation, 30–31, 114–15; kinds of, 47, 49; learning agility, *133*; on making money, 122–23; on people, 206; on personal responsibility and hard work, 206

Pert Plus®, 21, 25

physical development, 22–23, 62–65, *133*

pipeline, fitting product into, 104

pipeline, Serial Innovator, 147–49

planting seeds, 104–5

playing for high stakes, 109–11

"Pointy-Haired Bosses," 154

Polanyi, Michael, 81–82

politics. *See* organizational politics

positioning the product, 103

positive attitude, 99

potential business value, 103

potentially interesting problems, 42–46

potential Serial Innovators: zero to five years in industry, 141–43; five to ten years in industry, 143–44

power, organizational, 80, 107

pragmatic idealism, 161, 167–68

precision farming, 44–45, 57, 58–59

preparing to innovate, 32, 115–16, 129–33

preparing to understand, 47–48

problem(s): answering a different, 90; engaging with, 137–38; finding the right, 40–43, 46; first order effects of, 71; gaining understanding of, 47–52, 137; interesting, 39, 41, 45–46, 61–62, 144; reframing, 119; strategies to identify, 43–46; *vs.* opportunities, 41. *See also* interesting problems

process: finding and understanding, 40–48, 116–20, *133*; used by Serial Innovators, 32–34

Proctor & Gamble (P&G), 8, 21, 173, 183

product: competition from current line, 90; development pipeline, 104; expanding problems solved by, 86; line extensions, 16–18, 86; positioning within organization, 103; presenting and packaging, 84–86; staying with to commercialization, 87; understanding strategic context of, 103

Product Visionaries, 11

professional management, 153–54

profit, commitment to, 115, 124–25

profound understanding, 128–29, 206–7

project definition and acceptance, 22–23

project engagement skills, 137–39

prototypes and product demonstrations: Adam Gudat, 106–7; Tom Osborn, 85, 101, 107

purpose, 127

pushing the boundaries, 110–11

puzzles, love of, 116

qualitative modeling, 57, 59

quantitative data: aggregate market, 77–78; from modeling, 59

quilting exercise, 64, 101–2

radical innovation, 15

rage against ignorance, 117

Random Dot Stereograms, 82

rapport-building, 74, 101–2

recruiting by Serial Innovators, 100–101, 150–51
recruiting policies, unhelpful, 150
reframing problems, 44–45
reliability, 93
remotely-operated heavy equipment, 44–45, 57, 58–59
Rensselaer Radical Innovation Project, 20, 24, 27
repurposing, 55–56
reputation building, 92–93
responsibility, taking, 64–65
restenosis, 56
results orientation, 129, 206–7
reverse engineering, 51
reward systems, 159, 167
risk-taking: calculated, 111, 121; getting fired, 110–11; good and bad, 139; not with personal assets, 121–22
Rocket eBook®, 2
routine tasks boring, 127
rules, when to break, 110

salable interim products, 44–45
Sam (electronic device Innovator), 108
Sandra (consumer packaged goods Innovator), 60, 119–20
Science Applications International Corporation (SAIC), 154–59, 168–69
screened out during hiring, 149
seeds, 104–5
self-directed study, 116, 130–31, 144–45
selling to internal decision-makers, 98
sell simply while understanding profoundly, 102–3
seminars for product promotion, 85
Serial Innovators: characteristics of, 10, 112–34, 136–37; defined, 2,

12; described, 157–58; innovation process of, 33; lessons for, 86–88; love letter to, 186–87. See also managing Serial Innovators
shampoo/conditioner, 21, 25
silos/stovepipes, 155–56, 176
simplifying, 53, 59
skill sets of Innovators, 26
Skunk Works methods, 100
sleeping on a problem, 82
small firms, 152–53
Smarter Planet Research Initiative (IBM), 20
snowballing, 74
social networks, 93
soft/positive influence tactics, 99, 104–6, 139
solution, creating the, 81–83
Stage-Gate® new product development process, 17, 36, 62, 177
stakeholders, studying the, 103–4
start-ups, 152–53
stents, 56, 91
stories, 104–5
stovepipes/silos, 155–56, 176
strategic context, 103
strategic thinking, 103, 178–79
structural shifts, 182
subsidiary awareness, 82
suppliers, visiting, 80
support system, 95–96
Susan (paper products Innovator), 165
suspending judgment, 118–19
systems thinking, 58–59, 61, 114, 119–20, 131, 136, 203–4

3M, 163, 173
"Talent Rich and Innovator Light" companies, 147, 148
teams, assembling, 47–48, 54, 63–65, 80
technical managers, 161–68, 194–96

technical recruiting, 150
Technical Visionaries, 11–12
technology: knowledge in peripheral
   fields of, 32, 42, 45; as means to an
   end, 31, 123, 142
technology push initiatives, 19–21,
   27–28, 69
Ted (plastic wrap Innovator), 54
telling stories, 104–5
temporal directionality, 27
termination, risk of, 6–7, 110–11
Tesla Motors, 2
time constraints, 40, 87, 158–59,
   161–62
timing of innovation, 41, 104
tolerance for ambiguity, 42
trade-offs, 83–84
trade shows, 80, 143
trust-building, 91–94
T-shaped people, 130–31

unknowns, defining, 48
unsolved problems, 18–19

validating data, 60, 80–81
Valley of Death, 21, 24, 62
Valocchi, Michael, 20
variety, need for, 127
variety-seeking, 16
Victor Mills Society (Proctor &
   Gamble), 9, 173
Visionary, 11
visualization software, 106
voltage regulation, 43–44
volunteers, use of, 63–64, 102

weather inversions and pollution,
   78–79
white space, 110, 184
"why" questions, 75–76
wild ducks, 136, 141
workshops for product promotion, 85
worldview. See perspective

yogurt, 16

Zire, 16